Inclusive
Institut

INCLUSIVE DEVELOPMENT AND INSTITUTIONAL DYNAMICS

Rajesh Chatterjee
M.M. Semwal
Kashinath Jena

ABHIJEET PUBLICATIONS
DELHI 110094

ABHIJEET PUBLICATIONS
2/46 Tukhmeerpur Extension
Delhi 110094
Phones: 011-22960492, 65698474
e-mail: abhijeetpublication@gmail.com
abhijeet_singh1@indiatimes.com

INCLUSIVE DEVELOPMENT AND INSTITUTIONAL DYNAMICS

First Published 2008

ISBN 978-81-89886-63-9

PRINTED IN INDIA

Published by J.K. Singh for Abhijeet Publications, Delhi 110094, Lasertypeset by Gaurav Graphics, Delhi and Printed as Himanshu Printers, Delhi.

Foreword

No society or economy can aspire for sustainable growth and development without addressing the developmental issues at the bottom of the social pyramid. No doubt economic accomplishments in the context of India, particularly in the era of globalisation, have been spectacular but the debate is still going on about its nature, scope and beneficiaries. The million dollar question is how far Indian experimentation with the Top Down theories of development, have been accommodative of the aims and aspirations of the vast multitude of lesser souls, that are still scrawling in the periphery of a so called shining India. Do the ongoing developmental models have the intent and inclination to make the bottom of the social pyramid an equal stakeholder in the national prosperity? The answers are hard to come by, yet in the recent years a good number of researchers and policy makers have taken up with all seriousness, the issue of socio-economic exclusion and policy of inclusive development. To my reasonable satisfaction I find this volume titled 'Inclusive Development and Institutional Dynamics', co-authored by Dr. Rajesh Chatterjee, Dr. M.M. Semwal and Dr. K.N. Jena as most relevant and time-bound. Most importantly, the sincere care and concern shown by the authors towards the critical role of rural institutions in the domain of rural economic, political, cultural, educational and social development, is truly reflective and representative in character. Again, the thread bare and clinical analysis of the various weaknesses and strengths of the rural institutions vis-à-vis the rural empowerment is really comprehensive and commendable. By and large, I am quite optimistic of the acceptance of this book by both the academics and policy makers. I am also reasonably hopeful that this volume would go a long way in stirring up many a mind for further focused research in this field.

Prof. Amit Hazra
Director,
Rural Extension Centre,
Visva-Bharati, West Bengal.

Preface and Acknowledgements

Writing a book on developmental issues with a rural backdrop has always been a herculean task. However, to our good fortunes, we have received constant cooperation, constructive suggestions and continuous feed back from many a quarters that have immensely helped us to negotiate with the task of writing this book. And the result is that this volume could see the light of the day. Hence, no words would be suffice to express our gratitude to those selfless people but for whose cooperation and encouragement, we could have never accomplish our goal. With due acknowledgement, we take this opportunity to express our sincere thanks to our authorities, colleagues, well wishers and students in our respective universities (Tripura University and HNB Garhwal University) for their active supports to our modest endeavour. We have also the honour to express our gratefulness to all our peers who have been working in different universities and colleges for their timely feed back on our work and references. Our acknowledgment would never be complete without expressing our heart-felt indebtedness to Prof. Amit Hazra, Director, REC, Visva-Bharati (A Central University), who has been kind enough to go through our manuscript and written the foreword for this book. We are also grateful to Prof. Arunoday Saha, Hon'ble

Vice-Chancellor, Tripura University, Prof. S.P. Singh, Hon'ble Vice-Chancellor, HNB Garhwal University and Prof. C.P. Barthwal, Hon'ble Vice-Chancellor, Kumaun University, Nainital for their constant encouragement in our academic endeavour. To conclude we are also thankful to Sri J.K. Singh, the Managing Director of Abhijeet Publication, Delhi for publishing our manuscript.

Dr. Rajesh Chatterjee
Dr. M.M. Semwal
Dr. K.N. Jena

Contents

1

Introduction

Institutions may be defined as all those sectors, which contribute to an enhancement of human capital. Human capital refers to the fact that human beings invest in themselves through education, in-service training, nutrition and health so as to raise their life expectancy through lifetime earnings. As a logical sequel to the pursuit of this approach, a case for investment in these sectors is made using rates of return estimates. For example, in the education sector, which has been subjected to this type of analysis to a greater extent than health or nutrition, the available evidence from developing countries points to the fact that social returns to investment in primary education are more than twice the 10 per cent norm normally applied to opportunity cost of capital, higher for general education and women's education.

The impact of nutrition and health care has been measured at the micro as well as macro-levels. At the micro-level, health and nutrition enter wage relation, as inputs in the household farm and firm production function and also affect productivity in schooling and production function for children.

The human capital theory has been criticized on the grounds that it is narrow in approach and unlike the case of physical capital, is unable to consider asset prices in the analysis. It also neglects the influence of preferences of individuals, home consumption and production, social reproduction and schooling and health of family members.

More importantly, the theory views production as organized on an assembly line basis and ignores the role of human capital in creating new technology and new practices endogenous to economic units.

The new endogenous growth theory addresses itself to the last mentioned issue. Technological progress is not an exogenous factor influencing development but is the result of intentional actions taken by people who respond to market incentives. Since technology is considered to consist of a non-rival component, which is separate from individuals and can grow without bound, it leads to increasing returns to scale. Thus, private investment in research and development raises the level of technology so that it acquires the nature of a public good. Educated people not only use technology more efficiently, they are also likely to innovate and spread the benefits of such innovation to co-workers thereby increasing the efficiency of all factors of production.

The expected benefits of skills, knowledge, ideas and such other concepts emphasized by the endogenous growth theories can materialize only if the set of conditions that are necessary for translating individual level skills into enhanced productivity exist in the economy. This set of attitudinal and institutional characteristics, which is termed social capability, is a critical factor in economic development. In fact, economic development and social capability interact and influence each other in a cumulative manner, which indicates that initially inadequate social capability may frustrate growth and limit its own enlargement.

A more serious problem in applying the human capital as well as the endogenous growth theories based either directly or indirectly on the human capital approach is that it takes no cognizance of the pervasive and persistent poverty that is a characteristic feature of most developing countries, particularly in South Asia. Though income poverty severely limits the ability of individuals to invest in them, it does not form an integral part of the analytical frame of the human resource developers. Thus, the poor, the infirm and the disabled do not fall within the ambit of their analysis. Whether such a focus that leaves out between one-third to one-half of the population in developing countries out of the realm of analysis is relevant for policy formulation is a moot question.

Stiglitz317 (1995) pointing to the importance of the factor states the externalities and scale effects associated with human capital arise not just from the number of educated individuals, or from the number of years of schooling of each. India may have far more college graduates than Hong Kong. Rather, it arises from the patterns of specialization and interaction, which may arise; but whether these patterns of specialization and interactions do arise are matters of economic organization as well; they are affected, for instance, by patterns of industrial organization and social organization. Government may affect both. This cautions against the adoption of an excessively narrow interpretation of the impact of human capital on economic growth.

Human Development Approach

This approach emphasized providing for all people the basic means of well being which include among other things, food, health and education. The UNDP's human development concept emphasizing the enlargement of the range of people's choices goes much further than the concept of basic needs as it is based on functioning achievements rather than on commodity possession. The concept of human development encompasses empowerment, cooperation, and equity in basic capabilities and opportunities, sustainability and security. Restricting the scope of Institutions to only education, health and nutrition without tackling the cause for these deprivations would imply that the gains that are achieved in these spheres would be limited both in extent as well as duration. Sustained gains in human development can be made only if the poor have access to incomes and public policy facilities their access to education, health and nutrition, which in turn act to make the income distribution more egalitarian. In the absence of such a vision, the mutually reinforcing links between poverty, under nutrition, ill health and illiteracy would perpetuate the inegalitarian nature of development and could result in the phenomenon of social exclusion.

Social Sectors in India: Some Major Milestones

Up to the Fourth Plan, no specific programmes on social sector development were taken up. Social sector did not receive adequate priority. Whatever little was done, suffered due to lack of an integrated approach. The first major initiative towards social sector development began in Fifth Plan (1970) 261, with the launching of Minimum Needs Programme (MNP), which is a package including elementary education, health, water supply, roads, electrification, housing and nutrition. From then on the Minimum Needs Programme continued to be implemented in the country with some minor additions in the subsequent Plans. For instance, in the Sixth Plan Adult education was added to MNP and in the Seventh Plan, rural domestic energy, rural sanitation and public distribution system were also included as part of MNP.

The achievements were far lower than the need or requirement in the country. Further the quality of services was unsatisfactory. For instance, access to primary education is improved considerably, but illiteracy rate still remained high. As on date, more than half of the females and 37 per cent of males in the country are illiterates. Access to health services have also seen steady improvement, but birth rate, death rate, infant mortality rate and morbidity rates were far lower than the goals set in this regard. Coverage under water supply improved but the prescribed minimum 40 litres per day was not ensured. In view of this, Eighth Plan265 (1992-97) while continuing the MNP laid emphasis on quality in addition to quantity in MNP. Resources allocation in Eighth Plan was also stepped up towards MNP. In 1996, the Conference of the Chief Ministers identified seven Basic Minimum Services (BMS) and accorded high priority for implementation. A time bound Action Plan for various components of the BMS varying from 2-5 years was also finalized. The seven components of BMS are.

1. 100% coverage of PHC
2. Safe Drinking Water to all
3. Universal Primary Education
4. Housing to all shelter less
5. Nutrition support to children

6. Connectivity to all rural settlements
7. Revamping PDS with focus on backward areas.

However, political instability and frequent change of governments impeded any major achievements under BMS.

The translation of economic growth into enhanced capabilities for all lies at the heart of the development problem that faces a majority of low-income countries today. The role of what in economic parlance are called 'Institutions' is considered critical in this regard. Social sector activities are often considered to be those which emphasize improvement of quality of life by offering education, employment and health facilities to that part of the population, who are less privileged and who suffer from malnutrition, high death rates and disease, low income and lack of education and who live below the poverty level. Therefore, in summary, development involving the social sector has two important aspects:

i) Firstly, if involves 'quality of life' related activities and,
ii) Secondly, these activities are directed towards a certain section of the population, namely, the poor.

An alternative humanist development perspective called the Wage Goods approach to development was suggested by Kalappa, Narayana and P.R. Brahmananda (1987)47, but Pandit Nehru's romanticism of Soviet Socialism together with the euphoria of the international funding agencies for the big-push strategy of industrialization as the sine qua non of economic development of poor nations, had ensured the acceptance of the Mahalanobis strategy of development planning in our country pledging for the establishment of a 'socialist pattern of society'. The first U-turn in our development strategy took place in the middle of 1970s, when the actions on distribution were considered integral part of the strategies of growth, and explicit anti poverty programmes of various kinds were introduced with major funding by the central government and the state governments acting as primary implementing agencies. The issues of poverty, malnutrition, hunger, unemployment and the development of social infrastructure received priority in political and policy level discourses on development during this phase, which continued upto the end of 1980s. The second U-turn took place in 1991, when as per the tenors of the Washington Consensus, India opened the doors to globalisation, market-friendly reforms in her economic policies, downsizing the role of the state, adoption of structural adjustment policies for lifting the growth trajectory of the India economy, and enhancing the international competitiveness of her exports, while the issues of poverty eradication and alleviation of related endemic deprivations were relegated either to the trickle-down mechanism of growth in different sectors of the economy, or to the reduced form of government interventions in the name of targeting, and greater participation of NGOs. The Indian economy is presently going through this phase of development perception in a globalised economic scenario of sanctions, standards, and concern for human rights under global governance and directions. The response of economic agents to the change in economic environment can be evaluated in terms of choice of alternative criteria and the picture that emerges can be viewed either from the national angle or regional / state level or even the sub-regional or district levels. In this work we shall be focusing on the nature and extent of development in the Block with the Villages as the units of analysis or exposition.

Institutional Role

The Government of West Bengal, since 1977, has been propagating the use of an alternative model of development based on institutional reforms ensuring people's participation in the panchayats and local bodies, and introducing decentralized planning to effectively monitor and implement measures aimed at poverty alleviation, construction of social overheads, land reforms and empowering the people who had been historically deprived, like the backward castes and tribes, and the women. While there is some merit in such a claim to usher in institutional change related to the land and credit markets in the rural society of the state, and thus much of the progress in agricultural growth in the state in recent years have been attributed to such institutional change ensuring development from below, in many areas the progress has remained only perfunctory and unsatisfactory, as in many cases the panchayats and other local bodies have become extension counters of some government departments, with very little effective autonomy to chart out alternative development programmes independent of the design and control of the state government or even the central government. Many of the social progress measures that have been attempted through people's movement for freedom and expansion of capabilities have remained weak or marginal in their impacts, and in a globalised world, where the penetration of markets in different forms has threatened to sharpen asymmetries in rural and urban life in different parts of the country, there is urgent need to revamp the Panchayati Raj institutions in the progressive state of West Bengal. One of the fundamental difficulties in making our panchayats work as effective agents of socio-economic change in the changed economic environment has been the absence of suitable recording system, which is responsible for adhocism in the various development programmes undertaken and the consequent non-fulfillment of targets. As a result, we find that despite very tangible progress in the last quarter of the 20th century, the extent of deprivation for the population of West Bengal continues to be serious in terms of certain crucial indicators of progress and human development.

While inadequate resource allocation is a fundamental problem facing institutions, there is much that can be accomplished even within the existing resources.

Thus, there is enough evidence indicating that appropriate institutions go a long way in achieving rural transformation and in enabling the small and marginal farmers and landless labourers in overcoming the relative deprivation they suffer and the differential access to institutions they often undergo. What is keeping rural transformation at bay is not so much the absence of motivation for development, unwillingness to innovate on the part of people involved, lack of capital or appropriate technology per se, but is due to absence of appropriate institutions that really work to deliver the goods in 'the complex and uncertain world of economic relations.

There is enough evidence from rural India that the frequency use of services is not uniform through out the year and the services are not uniformly accessible to the people (Wanmali, 1976)369; that the services provided by the non-government agencies from spatially fixed (Wanmali and Ghosh, 1975)371, or spatially fixed but temporally mobile, locations are also capable of organising rural space; that there is room to look at the concepts of mobile service provision in rural India and that is some services such as regulated marketing of agricultural produce the government has created, rather than solved, problems by their introduction in rural areas.

Theories of growth poles, growth central places, spatial development and diffusion of innovations have attracted increasing attention as tools of development planning in both developed and developing countries. The appeal of these theories is well illustrated by the fact that their validity is assumed to be independent of the economic, social and political systems of the countries which wish to use them. An attempt is made, to note their characteristic features with a view to synthesising the various arguments put forward by the Indian experts in the past. The difficulty in undertaking to do this term not only from the interpretations of the concept in their original but also in their derived forms. For example economic space of one theory tends to become geographical space of another; a pole becomes a centre or a place; growth becomes development and vice-versa; rank size distribution becomes similar to the hierarchy of settlements; models of location of transportable commodities become those of immobile services, and the hierarchical organisation of interpersonal communication fields are sometimes confused with those of the complementary regions of central places. Further when these misinterpreted concepts are put into practice, the somewhat incorrect interpretations tend to add to the difficulty of understanding and of implementation.

It is maintained in the current literature on location theories and regional development that innovations (goods, services or outlets providing these goods and services) are passed down the successively lower levels of an urban hierarchy. At times, instead of trickling down the urban hierarchy, the growth tends to get concentrated in a few large cities and there opens up a wide gap between the big cities and their rural countryside (Berry, 1969)29. Such a gap, which is also a gap in the diffusion of innovations, is best dealt with; it is suggested, by creating more centres in the appropriate limb of the settlement system. Thus, it is argued that the role played by location theories, and particularly by the growth centres, is not insignificant in regional development. Indeed, close relationship has been found between the process of diffusion of innovations and the urban hierarchy (Pederson, 1970)275.

It becomes apparent that in the field of regional planning economic growth, and development was attempted to be achieved growth, and development, was attempted to be achieved through a variety of locational decisions within a region. Two approaches were followed; the industrial development approach which relied upon a more conventional growth pole and growth centre type exercises; and the development planning approach which was a programme for the creation of development infrastructure. The first approach was favoured by the developed countries to rejuvenate their backward regions and the second approach was a favourite of the developing countries of the Third World.

It will be, therefore, safe to say that there is no unified theory of regional development. An attempt, however, can always be made to analyse a regional development problem within the framework of a theory from one's own discipline and to complement that analysis, as far as possible, by looking at it from other points of view. For example, it would appear reasonable with the help of a growth pole or a growth centre type exercise; and those of service provision within the framework of a derivation of central place theory. In doing so, both the studies can take cognizance of relevant thinking on related problems such as spatial impact, process of diffusion and the socio-economic environment within which the studies are conducted. Such a comprehensive analysis, it is felt, would tend to enrich the understanding of the basic concepts rather than confusing them.

Most of the development theories have a spatial bias. Arthur Lewis (1955)208, a prime architect of the liberal democratic model, defined development as widening choices, in other words, greater economic prosperity to provide greater material comforts. The assumption was, as we stated earlier, that the growth would spread through the market forces and the state would provide social services and undertake other programmes to push the growth downwards. The expansion of economic wealth is expected to redefine the need, and the consequences may adversely affect the functioning of the democratic institutions. The ability of the state to develop the social services to expand education, health and employment and thereby bridge the already existing economic and social disparities is a crucial issue for debate. The use of new found economic and political power to end social discrimination is another important issue. The containing problem of the population growth coupled with mass illiteracy, economic deprivation and providing opportunities for economic participation are considered prime objectives of social development.

After nearly two decades of development efforts. Gunnar Myrdal (1968)238 and some other studies noted that the growth did not trickle down, the unemployment remained high despite economic growth, the population continued to grow at a high rate, the health and education standards were low and the growth of industrialization was leading to development of slums in the cities. As Streeten noted no theory helped in meeting adequate standards of nutrition, health and education, as it is not known precisely which financial, fiscal and human resources and policies produce these desirable results (Streeten, 1994)318. The discovery of these trends generated a lot of debate at different levels including international institutions.

Institutions and Credit System in India

Various government departments like Rural Development, Agriculture, Horticulture & Soil conservation, Fisheries, Forest, Tribal Welfare, Tribal Rehabilitation in Plantation and Primitive Group Programme, SC & OBC Welfare, Urban

Development, Education (Social Welfare and Education), Handloom, Handicraft & Sericulture are engaged in implementation of various central government as well as State Government projects through formation of SHGs with specific objectives and targets.

The state sponsored formal rural credit systems have a tremendous physical reach—through forty thousand rural and semi urban branches of commercial banks and RRB's and hundred thousand branches/ primary agricultural credit societies of cooperatives. Inaddition these systems have access to enormous resources, both in the form of deposits as also refinance assistance from NABARD and equity support from Central and State governments. Yet, as the earlier tables reveal, these systems have not been effective in serving the rural customers especially the poor.

This ineffectiveness appears to be linked to their organizational culture—which emphasizes values like target fulfillment, centralized control, and procedure bound approaches. The target orientation reduces the structures to delivery systems of Governmental subsidies. The rigid rules and procedures and impersonal relationships, makes the focus of the activities the rural branch—and not the rural poor households, who are spatially "outsiders". The limited share in the savings and credit market for the poor, with poor recovery, makes these operations, intrinsically unviable. The credit needs of the rural poor are organically different from that of other economic sections of society—which fact appears to have been overlooked in designing of strategies, structures and systems. Hence formal financial institutions play a limited role in the rural financial market, especially that of the poor. Few rural poor families continue a viable financial relationship with banks after IRDP loans—they usually are permanently out of the formal financial system because of their overdues from subsidized loans.

Poverty alleviation is the ultimate goal of all kinds of development in India. The planners took taken up several approaches for combating poverty during different plan periods. While most of the programmes failed to deliver the expected results, certain innovative efforts hold out fresh hope. One such effort is the formation of self help groups (SHGs) for enabling the poor to participate in the process of development in general and to come out from poverty in particular.

Almost all the promoters of development have taken SHGs as the only solution to eradicate global poverty. In India too, formation of SHGs became an ideal means for all the agencies like Government departments, Bankers, NGOs, civil bodies.

2

Review of Literature

In this chapter a brief review of the key word and concepts used in the study have been discussed. As the study is pioneering one in its own field, review is limited only to the content of the work.

The First Five Year Plan saw the introduction of the development programme in rural India. It was the first ever comprehensive attempt to solve the problems of rural areas in the Independent India. The programme itself was a mère listing of the priorities of rural development. It was launched in 1952, but on a pilot scale, to cover 52 community development blocks in the country. By the end of the Plan period, however, the entire country was covered by a network of the community development blocks. The programme was aimed at changing the attitudes of the people in rural areas and it hoped to prepare them for an era of rural development and planning (Mukherjee 1967)243.

In a country, may be rich or poor, institution plays a significant role which provides the basic ingredients, necessary for the survival of the mankind and also provides adequate raw materials which, when transformed as finished product is used as basic needs of human life. In a predominantly agrarian economy, this sector is envisaged as a strategic one, not only to provide food for teeming mass of the country but also as the generator of employment opportunities to them.

Human Development Approach

The human development approach puts people at the centre stage and supports measures to promote education, health and nutrition even if the conventionally measured rates of return on these investments are zero. Since the advocates of human development attach a higher importance to the supply of social services, particularly public services, the use of the concept also implies a greater role and responsibility for public provisioning.

Relevant in this context is the concept of social security whose connotation has been expanded in recent times from the conventional measures aimed at relieving economic and social distress due to specific contingencies such as death, old age and sickness, employment injury, maternity and temporary unemployment to encompass a whole range of measures including income generation programmes. Following Dreze and Sen (1989) 102, who advocate the pursuit of social security as an objective through social means, the definition of social security has been widened by researches to include maintenance of minimum levels of income. The distinction between the two sets of definitions of social security is sought to be made in terms of protective and promotional social security, with the ILO type measures constituting the former and direct anti-poverty measures, including asset distribution as well as employment generation programmes, provision of basic needs such as education, health, nutrition, housing for the poor and the like comprising the latter.

Following the approach, social sectors could be defined as those providing social security. The advantages of this approach, besides the more obvious one of linking the concepts of social sectors, social security and human development, would be that it provides a comprehensive framework which facilitates coordinated policy interventions for improving the state of human development. Indeed, it may be argued that the definition of social sectors cannot be divorced from the purposes for which such a definition is used. If the aim of human development is to enhance the capabilities of the bottom 40 per cent of the population, the two routes to such capability enhancement, viz., income generation and public provision of education, health and nutrition, cannot be divorced from each other. Infact, it is such a dichotomy in approach that explains the poor achievement on both fronts in most South Asian countries. In these countries characterized by pervasive poverty and consequent inequality of opportunities, restricting the scope of social sectors to only education, health and nutrition without tackling the cause for these deprivations would imply that the gains that are achieved in these spheres would be limited – both in extent as well duration. Sustained gains in human development can be made only if the poor have access to incomes and public policy facilities their access to education, health and nutrition which in turn act to make the income distribution more egalitarian. In the absence of such a vision, the mutually reinforcing links between poverty, under nutrition, ill-health and litcracy would perpetuate the inegalitarian nature of development and could result in the phenomenon of social exclusion.

The typology across countries shows that it is possible to achieve high human development at relatively low levels of income, the prime examples being Sri Lanka, Thailand, Colombia and Kerala in India. In fact, 37 countries in 1993 secured higher ranks on the Human Development Index as compared to their per capita income rankings (UNDP, 1996) 360. In order that growth and human development reinforce each other, greater attention needs to be paid to the pattern of growth. In the East Asian countries land reform and employment intensive growth formed the backdrop against which investment in education and health were undertaken Land reforms undertaken at the initial stages of development raised the incomes of the poor and enabled them to benefit form schooling resulting in improved enrolment and higher female literacy rates. A cross-section study of more than 80 countries indicates a strong negative relationship between basic education enrolment rates and the level of income inequality as measured by the Gini coefficient (World Bank, 1993) 374.

Similar findings hold true in the case of health as well. Anand and Ravallion (1993) 19 covering 25 developing countries with comparable data on poverty found that once the variation in the prevalence of poverty and per capita health expenditure by the government were taken into account, difference in per capita income became unimportant. Thus poverty reduction and government expenditure seem to be more important than income growth for attaining higher life expectancy.

The growing evidence that income inequality is harmful for growth also strengthens the argument that an equitable pattern of growth enables the attainment of high levels of social development. Empirical analysis shows that if South Korea in 1960 had Brazil's inequality, its GDP in 1985 would have been 15 per cent lower (UNDP 1996). 360

The emphasis on mass education led to a more equitable distribution of the benefits of education. Between 1960 and 1985 the premium that those with higher education could enjoy over those with only primary education declined from an additional 100 per cent to 66 per cent. This helped reduce wage inequality. In Brazil, education expenditure favoured the rich and the premium on higher education hardly changed (UNDP, 1996) 360.

Institutions in Indian Perspectives

In the context of Indian planning, the development of the institutions has always been an area of prime concern for planners, social activities, and academicians and therefore, figured at the core of five-year plans since its inception. In fact, its roots could be traced back to our rich glorious heritage where the state encouraged its subjects to develop progress and enhance their capabilities irrespective of their caste, creed, and gender by providing social assistance to vulnerable sections and promoting ideal and conducive environment (Dev, 1999) 97.

After attaining political independence, a number of statutory and socio-economic policy measures were adopted to improve the social sector by giving equal weightage to it just like the economic sector. The impact of planned efforts became more conspicuous on economic sectors where the nation emerged as a leader in many areas by achieving pathbraking success. For example, agriculture, sciences and technology, medicine, space research, to name a few, are some of the areas where the achievement level has been simply astonishing. However, on the social sector front, the progress achieved was relatively slower and its impact is a mixed one. In the case of education or literacy various field level studies show that though there has been an improvement in the overall levels of literacy, number of schools, number of students enrolled and number of teacher (Mehta, 1995) 212, yet there has also been a rise in the level of drop-out of students at the primary and middle levels (Majumdar and Vaidyanathan, 1994) 210, increasing marginalization of socially disadvantaged groups, dilution in the quality of education (Pillai258, 1992; Visaria, Gumber and Visaria365, 1993) and the high proportion of illiterates (Rahi, 1996) 279a. These are some of the illustrations that highlight the prevailing paradoxical situations. A number of studies reveal that such discrepancy is not only confined to rural-urban settings but is also conspicuous at inter-state levels. Likewise, for the health sector, it could be seen that there has also been a distinct improvement in the health indicators like the lowering of crude birth rate, crude death rate, infant mortality rate, enhancement in life expectancy at birth, largely on account of expansion in the infrastructure facilities. Unfortunately, this progress has, by and large, remained confined to the urban areas only whereas the situation in the rural areas still remains quite grim. Though several sub-centres, primary health centres and community health centres have come up in rural areas during all these plan periods, they are yet to be fully operationalized due to high incidence of absenteeism on the part of the doctors, paramedical and multi purpose staff. Generally, the absence of radiographers, lab technicians and other para medical professionals at these centres only adds up to their poor performance (Planning Commission, 1992-97) 265.

Similarly, the perusal of the performance in other social areas like poverty, housing, water supply, employment, etc., appears to be disappointing and lopsided. The uneven growth, with distinct tilt towards urban areas, has also accentuated the regional problems on the one hand and has also given impetus to the process of rural to urban migration on the other (Economic Survey, Govt. of India, 1992-93).

The limited success attained in the social sector could largely be attributed to the fact that it dealt primarily with the set of endogenous factors and values and their internalization by the people. The process, by its nature, is painfully long and slow. Therefore, social development takes a relatively longer time to become conspicuous than the economic development.

Service Centre planning is now regarded as an important tool to counter these anomalies, the initiation of a host of service centre programmes stands testimony to the fact that the government is quite concerned about the menace, thus for holistic development, development of both economic and service centre is vital because while economic development provides physical growth and prosperity, social development provides sustainability, which makes both the sectors complementary to each other. Thus, emphasis on one at the cost of others may be a source of disastrous consequences.

The apparent mismatch between the growth performance of the economic and service centres has resulted in various types of imbalances.

The connotation of the form social sectors varies depending on the user and the occasion on which it is used. Conventionally, the term is used to denote education, health and nutrition sectors, though in most countries with pervasive poverty, efforts to enhance social sector attainments rarely succeed without addressing the issue of poverty as well. However, most often in the appraised of policies pertaining to social sectors, the success or otherwise of various poverty alleviation strategies is usually not included.

Apart from the lack of a clear delimitation social sectors are rarely considered and analytical category and most of the analysis is generally confined to identifying the determinants and problems related to individual components such as education, health and nutrition. Thus, a critical of the problems relating to social sectors as an integrated whole is often missing.

Rural Disparities

V.G. Puranik (1970) 277, the Director of the National Co-operative Development Corporation, pointed out the significance of rural imbalances in the following manner: "Rural people form bulk of our population and their emancipation from evils arising from economic imbalances would depend upon how best we diversify out rural economy... Our strategy of economic growth has, therefore, to be such that it integrates rural and urban economies by eliminating regional imbalances."

In a detailed study of approach, strategy and perspectives of integrated rural development, S.K. Sharma and S.L. Malhotra (1977) 309 define this concept in the following manner: "Integrated rural development, thus, as a synergistic approach aims at total development of the area and the people by bringing about the necessary institutional and attitudinal changes and by delivering a package of services through extension methods to encompass not only the economic field e.g., development of agriculture and rural industries, etc., but also the establishment of the required special infrastructure and services in the area of health and nutrition, education and literacy, basic civic amenities, family planning, etc., with the ultimate objective of improving the quality of life in the rural areas."

R.P. Misra and K.V. Sundaram (1979)216, expressing their views on some aspects of rural development say that rural development means desired positive change in the rural areas—both in a quantitative as well as a qualitative sense. They define the concept in the following manner: "Thus, rural development is a real concept. It is a complete term which integrates a variety of human life and activities. We may broadly classify the numerous elements into the broad dimensions—social, economic, technological and natural. Rural development means desired changes in all these components. But such changes should take place in a mutually supporting relationship so as to generate organic and optimum development. Organic development is one which maintains a healthy relationship among the various elements or components of a system."

SHGs as Institution

The programme of linking self-help groups (SHGs) of the rural poor with the banking system was launched as a pilot project in 1992. Over the years the SHG-bank linkage programme has emerged as the major micro-finance programme in the country. 560 banks including 48 commercial banks, 196 RRBs and 316 co-operative banks are now actively involved in the operation of the programme. The programme has been providing the rural poor access to the formal banking system and has achieved several milestones in terms of gender sensitization, empowerment and poverty alleviation. The programme provides thrift linked credit support to the members of SHGs. While the programme directly benefits the members, it also helps banks in reducing their transaction costs as well as risk in delivering small loans. The Budget for 2004-05 has emphasized the need for promoting the programme more vigorously and for the graduation of the SHGs from consumption or production credit to credit for starting micro-enterprise. The Budget has set an indicative target of credit linking 5.85 lakh SHGs by end March, 2007.

The RBI has been taking a pro-active role in promoting micro-finance. It set up four Groups in 2002 look into various aspects of micro-financing. Based on the recommendations made by these Groups, the RHI announced that banks should provide adequate incentives to their branches in making procedures for financing the SHGs simple and easy. Based on the recommendations of the Vyas Committee, the RBI, in its annual policy statement for 2004-05, indicated that micro-finance institutions would not be permitted to accept public deposits, unless they comply with the extant regulatory framework (RBI, 2004-05). (Reserve Bank of India, Economic Survey, 2004-05)

Based on an economic paradigm—where poor women save regularly in a group fund, lend savings to members and finally link their fund to a bank for additional credit—SHGs form the backbone of good communication, governance and problem-solving in a community. While the model's benefits are many, its financial activities sustain and motivate SHG members to address community—identified needs in a number of areas. Examples of SHG initiatives in eastern India can be summarized as follows:

Self Help Group Initiatives are based on Education, Microfinance, Income Generation, Health, Sustainable Farming and Forestry, Civil Society, Watershed Management, Emergency Prevention (for recurring natural calamities), Social Evil Eradication and Peace (interfaith, interethnic, intercaste tolerance and conflict resolution) (NABARD, 2002).

> "(...) Voluntary association of persons self-motivated form common interest formed democratically without any political affiliations. Main objective is to improve economic and social status of its members as well as of the community. These are small homogenous groups (...) with mutual self-help attitude. Though not registered, but governed by an informal set of bye-laws framed by themselves. The strength of the group should be between 10-20 members. The main functions of the SHGs are to hold regular meetings, regular saving carry out community action programs, build up common fund". (NABARD, 2002)

NABARD conducted studies in the mid-eighties that brought out the simple fact that the most important and immediate banking needs of the poor households, in the order of their propriety were:

- Opportunities to keep safe their occasional small surplus in thc for of thrift
- Access to consumption loans to meet emergent needs and
- Hassle-free access to financial services and products, including loans for micro-enterprises

The studies also reveal that in the rural households of India, the economic resources and the discretion to utilize them are usually concentrated in the hands of male members. This concentration of economic power is one of the key reasons for the low prestige and weak bargaining position of women in the family.

A women members influence over the household's

economic resources has been defined here as her participation in/her ability to influence the decisions on the purpose of loan taken in SHGs, the adoption of household infrastructure programs, major household purchases especially the purchases of durables and occupational assets e.g., livestock, farm machinery, handloom, etc., occupational issues like which crop to sow or which seeds or other farm inputs to use, which supplier to buy the raw materials from etc., sale or mortgage of assets in times of financial need.

Financial Institutions

Finance is one of the most crucial inputs for economic activity, growth and development. If finance through own accumulated resource or equity is neither available nor sufficient, debt assumes a major significance. Financial institutions (FIs) play an important role in this regard by channeling funds from surplus sector (savers) to deficit sectors (investors). However, these institutions do not show much enthusiasm to put their resources in rural and backward areas for the benefit of poorer people as these are commercial organizations and are basically interested in profitability and sustainability, for two reasons: *(i)* incentive for functioning, and *(ii)* for safeguard the interest of stakeholders. Besides, the transaction in credit market is different from the transaction in goods market (Llanto, 1990). Unlike in the latter where transaction ends with the sale of goods and receipt of payment, which are more or less instantaneous, in the former what is important is the future endowment of the borrower which depends upon the purpose of the loan, viability of the project and creditworthiness and the strategic skill of the borrower. As these rural backward areas lack infrastructure, entrepreneurship, opportunities, and people are victims of exploitation and ignorance, the transaction cost of investment by the financial institutions and credit risk are high, and return on capital by borrowing investors is not attractive.

Besides, rural economic agents find the formal urban institutions alien and inaccessible, the attributes, characteristics and personal circumstances of the rural agents are not very much acceptable to the Formal Financial Institutions (FFIs). For both information gap exists. This accentuates the problem for the FFIs to locate both a good borrower and a good project. Borrowers know themselves better than the FFIs, but do not desire to fully disclose all relevant personal and project information (Leland and Pyle, 1977). The information transfer is hampered by serous moral hazard and incentive problems (Llanto, 1990).

Any modern government, however, does not like to deny economic development to the rural areas because of either strong linkage between agricultural and industrial development or political advantage. Credit reform becomes imperative as credit programmes are easier to implement than other policies (Braverman and Guasch, 1989). Therefore, if the FFIs lack the Schumpeterian entrepreneurial quality to innovate in the rural areas on their own, they are directed to operate there. Whatever be the reason for entry, formal institutions during the course of economic development are likely to expand faster than informal institutions and are expected to take over the part of the latter's function (Holst, 1985); hence informal financiers and loan association become redundant (Drake, 1980).policy makers try to provide cheap credit as an alternative to moneylenders or informal institutions in order to curb their monopoly power and high interest rate charged by them (Hoff and Stiglitz, 1990). It is however doubtful whether such a policy either improves access to credit for the poor or eliminated moneylenders or reduces interest rates (Bell, 1990) charged by them.

An ambitious credit scheme; 'Integrated Rural Development Programme' (IRDP) with a considerable element of subsidy was launched to alleviate poverty. It is doubtful whether alleviation of poverty and creating a strong rural market were the major motives behind it. So corruption and leakage became the central point. The IRDP borrowers were considered as 'Passengers' in the banking bandwagon, and less than 10 percent of them have been found to be still associated with the banks after their loan 'repayment ' was over (Pulley, 1989). Besides corruption, the programme was ill-conceived to boot. It was a supply-led not demand-led credit programme so that the clients did not have choice over 'purpose' and 'amount'; entrepreneurial skill was assumed which was not there; backward and forward linkages were never of any concern during implementation. Credit target was the main concern and bureaucratic machinery was in charge of ensuring the credit achievement for which they did not have any professional respect. The FFIs were not allowed to apply the principle of three Cs: (I) Character, meaning how a person has handled past debt obligations, (II) Capacity, meaning current available assets of the borrower can comfortably handle, and (III) Capital, meaning current available assets of the borrower, such as real estate, savings or investment that could be used to repay debt if instalment/ income should be unavailable. It is not that the public sector financial institutions were very unhappy about the situation as they did not disburse these loans with a sense of commercial viability but dispensed it with disdain as a 'social obligation' and to attract government's favour elsewhere. So the top management never accepted this as a challenged and rural branch managers disbursed credit with indifference. Theses loans were written off from the psychological ledger of the bankers on day one. Agriculture and Rural Debt Relief (ARDR) scheme further hardened the attitude of the bankers towards rural credit, and the rural borrowers towards repayment. As on story goes, on one occasion a woman borrower in response to a Minister protested that she had not taken a *sala* (loan in Kannada, an Indian language) from a bank but agreed that she had taken a bank loan. Whereas a *sala* is a loan bound by traditional sanctions and norms and is always returned, the bank loan is a 'gift' from the government (Fernandez, 1998). Distribution of cheap and easy loans without any respect for repayment seemed more important (Bouman, 1989). All these only weakened the strength of the financial institutions to serve the poor and the rural areas, and further reduced their interest to transact such business. Although moneylenders became less important alter Independence due to government intervention, they have started reassuming an important role in recent years largely due to the poor quality of institutional credit (Rajsekhar and Vyasulu, 1990). Besides, there was an urgent need for financial innovation in the credit market as there was no certainty about the completion of a credit transaction (Bhatt, 1987). This is a story not only of India but of many of the developing countries.

Micro-credit as an alternative source of credit for the poor has received wide attention in recent years. It is defined as "programs that provide credit for self-employment and other financial and business services (including savings and technical assistance to) to very poor persons" (World Bank, 1997).

Micro-credit institutions evolved their own design features such as class eligibility for membership in the group ranging from landless to minimum land holdings; prior entrepreneurial experience to no requirement of entrepreneurial experience; monthly repayments to collateral to no-collateral; and group lending contracts to no-group lending contracts. These institutions remain most successful ones in terms of: *(a)* outreach and performance in delivering credit services to the poorest of the poor women and small artisans in the rural and urban areas; *(b)* reduction in adverse selection of borrowers; *(c)* development of collateral substitutions; *(d)* offering cost effective approaches to formal institutions (Yaron, 1994; Besley, 1994); *(e)* behavioural outcomes such as non-land asset hodings by women, male and female labour supply, household expenditure and boys and girls schooling (Pitt and Khandker, 1998), and *(f)* empowerment of women (Kabeer, 2001).

The group formations under micro-credit institutions are based on a growing institutional concept in terms of resources and management skills of the women members to reduce the gender inequality and to increase their confidence to get involved in issues and programmes in the public and private spheres. The success of group lending is attributed to various factors such as the ability of the group to mitigate symmetric information problems in the credit markets through active screening of members; information advantage of the groups about the applicant's creditworthiness; social cohesion and heterogeneity of asset holdings; self-selection or assortative matching of members ; social ties between borrowing group members; group pressure to repay the loans; and peer monitoring through intra-group insurance. (Wenner, 1995).

Market as Institutions

The structure of rural financial market in India is dualistic; both formal and informal financial intermediaries. A consensus is growing among researchers that the formal financial sector is not effectively serving the rural population in the Third World countries (Bouman, 1984). This is mainly attributed to the failure of financial intermediaries in fulfilling their basic functions, viz., production credit to finance income generating activities, consumption credit to maintain and expand human productive capacity, and quality saving schemes for increasing risk-hearing capacity of the rural households. Moreover, these institutions have failed to promote any of its social objectives (Desai and Namboodiri, 1996). To reach the poor, institutional innovations are needed that enable services to be expanded, while substantially reducing transaction costs for both financial institutions and clients (Zeller and Sharma, 1998). In many countries in the world micro-credit programmes have succeeded in generating self-employment by providing access to small capital to people living in poverty (United Nations, 1998).

The performance of formal financial institutions particularly in their lending to the poor in India has been unsatisfactory. They face a number of constraints in broadening their services to the poor. A large number of rural households are with limited land resources and small economic activity accompanied with poor technology. But their demand for credit has been rising due to growing family size, increased consumption requirements, social obligations and so on. But the institutional agencies not only lacked the required mechanism to assess their credit needs but often overlooked their demand for credit on the ground that their needs are for non-productive purposes. Besides, perceived high risks, transaction costs in small scale rural lending and absence of collateral securities kept the poor away from the fold of formal financial intermediaries.

There has been a surge of interest in micro finance in the recent past, particularly in the context of reaching the poor families in a more effective way (Kaladhar, 1997). The importance of micro finance as an effective vehicle of alleviating poverty, especially in rural areas through the empowerment of women is now widely recognized. There are several methods of operating a micro finance project. The successful experience of a public sector bank, without the involvement of either the Government or any non-Government organization (NGO) in India is discussed here. Some suggestions for further improvement, based on the experience of certain other similar projects are also made. As an informal supplementary credit delivery mechanism by lending at group level, the Self Help Groups (SHGs) came into existence.

Non-Government Institutions

Rajesh Chakraborti in his article "Micro Finance in Eastern India—A Case Study" opines that NGOs are promoting and linking about 75 per cent of all the Indian SHGs to the formal banking sector. While delving into the working experience of an NGO named "Bagaria Relief and Welfare Ambulance Society (BRWAS)" located in the South 24 Parganas District of West Bengal, the author shows that an NGO can really work towards improving the condition, economic as well as social, of poor people in the country. As a micro-finance institution, the BRWAS organizes people into SHGs, help them develop a regular saving habit, provides "inter-loans" from the funds generated from these savings and more importantly, acts as an intermediary between banks and SHGs. The NGO has formed 106 SHGs under the SGSY scheme and about 159 SHGs under its Swanirvar Scheme. Most of the SHGs formed by this NGO are engaged in agriculture, animal husbandry—dairy (cows) and poultry and fishing. The presence of banks and moneylenders do not produce any threat to the NGO because of its credibility and deep level of trust among the common people. The NGO maintains an extensive management information system through its widespread network of volunteers as well as its close rapport with the villagers. In sum, the author through this paper offer the message that organizational sustainability including employee retention and motivation is a key issue in the long term effectiveness of an NGO.

Vina Mazumdar in her report, "Peasant Women Organise for Empowerment: The Bankura Experiment" presents the experience of the Centre for Women's Development Studies (CWDS) association with groups of poor peasant women in Bankura District of West Bengal. The author points out that organizing rural workers is a difficult task in general because of the intermittent and scattered nature of the work and their general helplessness. The report argues that organization of poor women is a vital instrument not only for equity but also to expand the base for women's participation in development. The study was conducted in Ranibandh block of Bankura District which has a large concentration of tribal population. In the opinion of the author, the greatest lesson from the Bankura project was its ability to promote collective participation to transform or transcend women's narrow identities. The experiment gives the message that taboos on inter-communal social relations, eating together, marriage choices, speaking in public, accepting leadership of a person that are considered to be lower in social status seem to break down more easily when the women act together. The author says that there are clear indications of a growing awareness on the part of some sections within the Government and the leaders of the local representative bodies that organized groups of women workers can represent a force in development.

The study brought out that SHG-bank linkage programme pioneered by NABARD and partnered by banks, NGOs and government agencies has emerged as a primary microfinance service mechanism for the unbanked poor in India. The multiple initiatives led by capacity building have encouraged bankers to view SHG-banking as a new dimension of quality portfolio with very low risks and with marginal increase in operating costs. The dimension and flexibility of SHG banking practised in India is now unmatched in the world's banking system. Being predominantly women focussed, SHG-banking is the first step towards feminisation of the (micro) banking portfolio of Indian banks. Stimulating self-help capacity of the poor does spark off the entrepreneurial enthusiasm and risk mitigation mechanisms in low income households. It also serves as an entry-road to overcome poverty and addressing other crucial social concerns. (Dr. Erhard W. Kropp, Dr. B.S. Suran)

Micro-Credit Institutions

As micro credit organizations faced the problem of lack of collateral, and high transaction costs involved in loan appraisal, monitoring and enforcement, group-based forms of lending originated as solutions to the twin problems. As Dichter puts it, in theory the group serves as a set of co-guarantors, operating through peer pressure and the group member's incentive to keep each other solvent so that they themselves do not lose the opportunity to receive a loan. The group serves also as a way to get around imperfect information, since members of the group know each other. Thus the transaction costs involved in loan appraisal are reduced if not eliminated (Dichter T, 1999).

The challenge in group-based programmes has to do with the other side of solidarity; solidarity can work both on the way "down" as well as on the way "'up". It is because of this, that we are seeing instances of the "domino effect" where one member defaults and the others follow. And ironically, when groups are most solid, in the sense that the members really come from the same small locale, and share the same kinds of economic activities, co-variant risk, often leading to group default, is greater. More important still, is the insight from one Bangladesh study that group defaults can itself be a function of group success. A group-based microcredit scheme operated by BRAC in Bangladesh was deemed successful—"as measured by increases in income of the members". But because of the increased income, the nature of the relationships in the group, and the culture of the group begin to change. Because not all persons in the group are the same, and not all 'life chances' are the same, not all the members of the group prospered in the same way. Some became gradually better off than others. A researcher studying the programme showed that some members with new income begin to feel that they had less to lose by ignoring group pressure to repay, and thus became defaulters, as a function of the new power of their money, rather than because of their inability to repay (Dichter, T, 1999).

Khandker (1998) estimated that for every 100 taka lent to a woman, household consumption increases by 18 taka; this figure is 11 taka if the same amount was lent to a man. Controlling for other factors for BRAC members upto three years, it was seen that moderate poverty fell by around 15 per cent and ultra poverty by 25 per cent. These results suggest that the poverty reduction impact of credit declines with cumulative loan size for BRAC. Khandker's results are more intuitive in the case of the two other microcredit programmes in his study, Grameen and Bangladesh Rural Development Board, where the rate of reduction in the incidence of poverty increases with cumulative loan size (Zaman, 1999).

The impact of credit on women's empowerment is contested. One set of opinion uses empirical data to prove that credit programmes contribute positively to women's empowerment, while on the other hand; a skeptical viewpoint believes that such programmes do little to alter gender relations and in fact sometimes contribute to reinforcing existing gender imbalances. It is also indicated that automatic benefits to women cannot be assumed even in the most innovative of programmes (Mayoux L., 1997).

Goetze, Anne Marie and Rita Sengupta (1996) have also questioned the naivety of the assumption that economic empowerment is a straightforward process, and easing women's access to credit translates unproblematically into their control over its use. As Mayoux puts it, impact on empowerment cannot be inferred from takeup of financial services or repayment levels. Women may repay through taking loans elsewhere and getting into serious debt. In many cases, the loans have been used by men to set up enterprises over which women have little control. In some cases they have even been employed as unpaid family workers with little benefits (Mayoux L., 1997).

A summary of "micro-enterprise" characteristics from the literature on the informal sector shows that most "microenterprises" are generally one person; got started using own savings, or money borrowed from family; find easy entry into the marketplace; are low skill; experience low or no growth even with financial services; have high death rates (go out of business); have low productivity; operate out of home or are mobile; sell whatever they make or serve directly to the consumer, operate in a market with very high levels of competition (for women this competition is even fiercer); which operate in "manufacturing", are in fact engaged in "making and repairing things" of low quality and low value; and which operate in trade are involved in low margin street vending and food services. While in terms of percentages, micro-enterprises can benefit from microcredit (being able to buy 50 kg of rice to sell instead of 25 kg is a 100 per cent increase in stock); such a change does not necessarily make the product more competitive, or alter the conditions in the marketplace. "Nor does such credit necessarily move the clients forward economically, even when, and perhaps especially when, surrounding conditions begin to improve." Microenterprises are not likely to remain viable in any context that begins to be economically well articulated, dynamic and competitive on the bases of skill and quality. And such a context is increasingly pervasive in this age of "globalization".

3

Research Methodology

Sampling Design

For the purpose of the study on Institutional Dynamics, it is imperative to choose such an area where disparity can be traced on the basis of Institution. Many of the social progress measures that have been attempted through people's movement for freedom and expansion of capabilities have remained weak or marginal in their impacts, and in a globalized world, where the penetration of markets in different forms has threatened to sharpen asymmetries in rural and urban life in different parts of the country. There is urgent need to revamp the rural development institutions in the progressive nation.

Growth and development in west Bengal and Tripura have not been uniform among districts, and it has gradually led to a marked regional imbalance. The states has laid major thrust on improving literacy level, but the drop-out rate is still high; the highest being among the Schedule Tribes. Although medical and health-care facilities have been expanded vastly, they still remain woefully short of requirement. The database on health-care facilities is poor and information on medical and paramedical staff is scanty and unreliable. The states' position have deteriorated as neither industry nor agriculture has improved in terms of production or productivity. The incidence of poverty is more extensive in rural than in urban West Bengal & Tripura, and 27.6 and 39 percent of the population is below the poverty line.

Birbhum district of West Bengal and West District of Tripura are chosen on the basis of Human Development Index (HDI).

The Villages of these districts have been selected on the basis of basic amenities available in the block and this block stood first among the 19 blocks.

The survey method followed to collect primary data is complete enumeration of service centres in every Gram Panchayat and household survey of the villages to find out the receivers of services from different Institutions. Each and every household of these villages has been interrogated about their socio-economic status in the villages with the help of pre-framed schedules and questionnaires. Total 480 households (80 households from each village) have been taken randomly as the samples from the four villages for the study. In the present study all these households have been treated as the primary units of survey.

Study has also been made to find out the importance of the Institutions on the more developed villages (MVs) and less developed villages (LVs) by adopting:

1. Focus Group Discussion
2. PRA Method
3. Semi Structured Interview (SSI)
4. In-depth Interview

PRA method, Semi Structured Interview (SSI) and In-depth Interview have also been carried out in every sample villages.

Analytical Procedure

Frequency of occurrence of service centres along with their distances has been counted. It depicts for multi-dimensional growth and structural changes in social systems, a new strategy of focusing attention upon certain favoured places to achieve wider regional goals is now being increasingly advocated in many countries. These favoured places have been variously termed as growth poles/centres/points/ nodes. The growth-pole model in empirical analyses seeks to provide a conceptual framework for regional development by identifying centres which have the capacity to induce growth and development in their hinterlands by generating sustained and long duration development.

As a lower level hierarchy in the growth-pole model, we can identify growth or service centres, which provide a package of the goods and services that is necessary for integrated rural area development.

It aims at the identification of growth poles and centres and the provision of requisite socio-economic infrastructure, viz. credit facilities, market network, bus service, extension service, communication system, health, marketing system and educational facilities at the proper centres which is considered to be the crucial variable in rural area development.

For the identification of growth and service centres in the study area, the method used by the David M. Smith (1972) has been adopted.

Smith's method requires the derivation of a single general indicator or a restricted set of indicators measuring major dimensions of the concept. This necessitates the combination of data on different conditions. This method has the added advantage of being rooted in the concept of "Service Centres".

In the present study, the selection of variables has been done on the understanding of the concept of centrality in the rural context and the available literature of the subject.

ii) Notional tabulation and percentage methods and the structured interview, semi structured interview, focus group discussion and PRA (Participatory Rural Appraisal) methods have been used.

Techniques of Interviews

Structured Interview

Structured interviews are usually based on pre-designed questionnaires filled by an interviewer. In the strictest quantitative tradition, interviewers working with quantitative interview schedules try to use exactly the same wording, prompts and tone of voice for each interview, to ensure that every interview is conducted as similarly as possible. Nowadays computer interviews provide the closest approximation to this ideal. In an interview situation with two human beings involved, it is virtually impossible to make each interview the same. This has its advantages, even in quantitative designs. The added flexibility of an interview allows misunderstandings to be clarified, and enables the researcher to ensure that the right person answers the questions in the right orders. None of these advantages are available in mailed questionnaires.

The general rules for structured interviews follow the same principles as for questionnaires. Depending on the design of the study, it is often possible to include more open-ended questions in structured interviews than in mailed questionnaires, as the interviewer can prompt the respondent, probe for more information, and clarify what the questions mean. Structured interviews can also be longer than mailed surveys, as respondents will be more motivated to talk with interviewers than to complete lengthy pen and paper exercises, and there is less concentration involved if the interviewer is recording the answers.

Semi-Structured Interview

As the name implies, semi-structured interviews fall somewhere between structured and in-depth interviews. Usually semi-structured interviews follow a set outline of topics with some pre-tested questions and prompts in each section. These are the triggers for the main directions of the interview and interviewers are mostly required to at least ask the questions on the schedule as they appear. However, having asked a particular question and recorded the answer(s), the interviewer is often allowed to explore additional information that the respondent has raised, to ask other questions, or to follow up issues that were not originally included in the interview schedule.

Thus, the interviewer is allowed more initiative and has more ability to respond to the perceptions and priorities of the respondent. Semi-structured interviews vary enormously in the degree of structured and amount of initiative, which is given to the interviewer. They can be ideal research instruments for exploratory and descriptive designs in which the researcher is finding out about a topic and/or has little prior knowledge of what the respondents think about it. Skilled interviewers are needed for semi-structured interviews because so much depends on the interviewer's ability to pick up, explore and accurately record additional information.

Typically, semi-structured interview schedules contain many open-ended questions, with lots of suggestions for prompts and probes. Probes can include summary techniques, in which one can summarize what the person has said and controlled non-directive probing in which one can ask further questions. It is important to leave plenty of room on the page under appropriate headings for the extra information interviewers may collect. Sometimes semi-structured interviews are audio-recorded but due to the costs of transcription, it is more usual for the interviewers to record the responses on the interview schedule.

In the semi-structured interview gender, age, class and ethnicity of interviewers can heavily influence how the respondent answers questions. This is more of an issue in face-to-face interviews than in mailed surveys or telephone interviews in which the characteristics of the interviewer may not be as obvious.

In-depth Interview

In-depth interviews are the most flexible type of research instrument and are used in qualitative research. Generally the researcher(s) conduct in-depth interviews themselves rather than employing other interviewers. This is because the quality of data collected depends, so much on the skill of the interviewer and their developing understanding of the issues, which they are researching. Whereas semi-structured interviews include many open-ended questions, in-depth interviews are often seen as being more of a discussion, and ideally are guided by the respondent rather than the interviewer.

The structure of in-depth interviews depends on the nature of the topic, the context of the interview and the personality and skills of the researcher and the respondent. Although at one end of the spectrum of in-depth interviews it is theoretically possible to begin with absolutely no structure other than a general topic, most researchers arrive at in-depth interviews with a number of topics or areas that they wish to cover and a loose structure for how they anticipate the interview unfolding. This enables some comparison of what different respondents think about the same issues. It is also important, for ethical reasons, to be able to foreshadow the general content of the interview and the way it will be conducted, in order for the respondent to give their informed consent to the research.

During an in-depth interview and in follow-up interviews, new issues, which emerge can be fully explored. The aim of an in-depth interview is to see the world from the eyes of the respondent as much as possible, to explore with them their thoughts and feelings and to thoroughly understand their point of view. Whatever structure is planned before the interview is less important than capturing the 'reality' of the person being interviewed, including their own language and use of words.

A critical skill in in-depth interviewing is the ability to establish a relationship with the respondent in which they feel free to openly express their inner thoughts and feelings. The skill of demonstrating empathy, in which the person being interviewed feels heard, accepted and understood, is vital to in-depth interviewing. Empathy is a complex skill which involves the researcher's own characteristics (age, gender, socio-economic status, etc.) as well as learned communication skills. Communication skills involved in empathy include attending to the respondent's verbal and non-verbal messages, displaying attentive, respectful listening, and accurately reflecting back the content and feeling of what has been said, including the 'message beneath the message'. Accurate empathic listening is a powerful way to help respondents' clarity what they think and feel, to explore it in more detail and to become more specific. Empathy can be built up over several interviews.

Clearly, given the nature of in-depth interviews, the researcher must have exceptionally good interviewing skills, a highly developed theoretical understanding of research methodology, and considerable experience in this method before they attempt it without close supervision. Researchers using in-depth interviews can experience high levels of stress, which can adversely affect the quality of the data they collect.

Focus Group Discussion

Interviews can also be conducted with groups of people. Focus groups are groups that parallel the range of interviews, from semi-structured to in-depth interviews. Structured interviews are also often administered in groups, but these are not focus groups because the role of the interviewer is to administer the questions on the questionnaire, and the role of the respondents is to answer the questions as presented.

In focus groups the researcher is usually prepared with some structure, a list of topics and trigger questions, but also aims to use the group discussion to explore the topic further. People in the focus group are often specially chosen because of their interest, involvement or knowledge in relation to the research issue. The group process during the discussion allows people to develop their ideas with each other, and to 'brainstorm' different options or opinions. With skilled facilitation, focus groups can come up with ideas and solutions which none of the individual members had thought about beforehand. Focus groups can be an economical means of gathering data. On the one hand, they can produce creative ideas; on the other, 'group think' can operate so that individual members feel afraid to voice their true opinions and diversity is lost. Much depends on the skill of the group facilitator.

Participatory Rural Appraisal (PRA)

Participatory Rural Appraisal (PRA) approaches have become increasingly popular for participatory development. Such approaches are based on post-positivism and combine the strengths of "constructivist" paradigm and that of "critical realism". From the "constructivist" paradigm, PRA approaches seek to understand human experience as it is

INSTITUTIONAL VENN/RANKING

To understand how the institutional arrangement for Rural Development and Poverty Alleviation worked, resort was taken to the Institutional Venn/ Ranking. The Institutional Venn/ranking are the visual method to represent the role of institutions and the degree of their importance in decision-making. The process was as follows.

The group wrote down the names of all the institutions, which had a bearing on their lives and their village. After consulting among themselves, they made a list of the institutions. Names of the institutions were written on separate pieces of paper and in different sizes; making such that one piece of paper bore just one name. Then they were requested to paste the institutions in order of their importance to the community according to their best judgment.

This is also a method of quantifying qualitative information obtained from the field data. Through Venn diagram, the rankings of social institutions have been marked carefully and then the entire process has been converted into the ranking and plotted against ranks by taking individual study villages. The unique feature of quantifying this qualitative data into quantities has been attempted in this study is pioneering one in the field of PRA/PLA methods.

BODY MAPPING

To know the overall health status of the members of the groups Body Mapping technique had been used. Often an outline of a human body is mapped for health-related discussions During group discussions such body mapping helps in highlighting different parts of the human body, which are causing problems. It is an effective "visual" medium for carrying on conversations on health-related issues like skin disease / stomach related problems and others. The common health problems have been listed and ways have been discussed for handling them.

DISEASE CENSUS

This method is used to identify the communicable and

lived and felt by the participants, the context of such experience in an interdisciplinary framework.

In a short period of time, PRA as a methodology has attracted attention and strengthened itself through its emphasis on the people's capabilities, field-based learning and innovations. Many experts have realized that the time has come for reversing their roles, as facilitators of development, where the weak, deprived and marginalized people are able to express their own views and do their own analysis in their own ways with the help of PRA process methods. PRA has supported the paradigmatic shift in the world of development and has helped to fill the vacuum existing in the sphere of social development methodologies.

Techniques of PRA

Tools/Techniques used

PIE DIAGRAM

Pie diagram or pie chart has been adapted as a PRA method to visually depict proportions of the constituents in relation to the whole. Some also refer to it as Chapatti Diagram. Chapatti diagram, however, is more commonly used to refer to Venn diagram.

Pie diagram is a simple method used to represent the relationship of various constituents to a whole. Pie diagram in other disciplines is used as a tool to present information in a visual form based on factual data. In PRA, pie diagram is used more as a method to help the local people to arrive at the constituents of a whole and also their proportions rather than just as a presentation tool. In contrast to its usage in other disciplines, pie diagram in PRA deals with both factual and perceptual data.

With the help of Pie chart method the following information has been collected in PLA

1. Income Status:
2. Expenditure Pattern

non-communicable diseases prevail in the study area. This method is helpful to identity the diseases from the rural people with an easy method comfortable to them and easily understandable. This is a new innovation adopted in PRA for this study.

Communicable Diseases:

Communicable and infectious diseases constitute a major cause of premature death in rural areas. Despite significant progress achieved in the overall quality of life, the proportion of total deaths on account of communicable diseases, maternal and prenatal conditions, and nutritional deficiencies continue to be unacceptably high.

The communicable diseases found in the study area are:

Malaria, Tuberculosis (TB), Hepatitis (Jaundice), Lymphatic Filaria, Leprosy, Sexually Transmitted Diseases (STDs), Dysentery, Diarrhea, Whooping Cough (pertussis), Small Pox, Mumps (Epidemic parotitis), Malaria, Measles, Giardiasis.

Non-Communicable Diseases

Health transition, whereby Non-Communicable Diseases become the dominant contributor to the burden of diseases, is principally due to a combination of demographic and lifestyle changes resulting from socio-economic development. Demographic transition is characterized by changes in population age structure with decline in fertility and an aging population. As more individual survive upto middle age, the years of exposure to the risk factors of chronic disease increase. The non-communicable diseases consist of cardiovascular diseases, cancers, diabetes, neuropsychiatry ailments, respiratory diseases, and other chronic diseases and injuries in any form. Addictions such as Tobacco and Alcohol aggravate the burden of diseases.

The non-communicable diseases prevalent in the area are: Ulcer, Typhoid, Anemia, Hemorrhage, Peptic Ulcer, Gastritis, Stomatitis, Hiatus Hernia, Tetanus, Ascariasis, Epidemic Dropsy, Diabetes Mellitus, Rickets, Thalassaemia, Common cold, Laryngitis, Tumor, Pneumonia, Appendicitis,

Bronchitis, Blood Pressure, Alcoholism, Gastric ulcer, Hysteria, Leukemia, Tropical Eosinophillia, Cholera, Meningitis, Arthritis, Cancer.

How to make a body map is stated below:

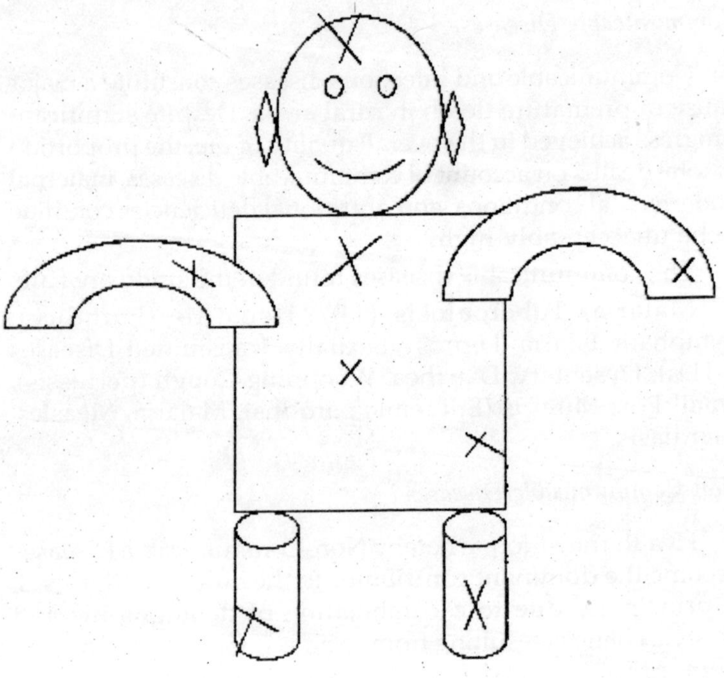

CONVERTED PIE

To quantify and consolidate the qualitative information obtained from the study area, quantifications of data has been done by converting the field diagrams (pie diagrams) into degree units and then percentage analysis has been done on that basis. Hardly any PRA practitioner used this conversion for the sake of explanation and simplicity for the researchers' in the field of rural development.

4

Demographic Features of the Study Area

Tripura

Tripura was declared a full-fledged state on 21st January 1972, under direct administrative control of the Government of India. The state a land locked hilly state in the north-eastern India is surrounded by Bangladesh almost on all sides except an out let by the north-eastern side through Karimganj District of Assam and Aizwal district of Mizoram in the East. The state is situated between 22°56′ and 24°32′ N latitudes and 91°09′ and 92°20′ East longitudes. Its maximum extreme length measures about 183.5 km from North to South and extreme width about 112.7 km from East to West. Its border with Bangladesh, Mizoram and Assam are 856 km, 109 km and 53 km respectively.

Administratively, the state is divided into four districts, namely, Dhalai, West Tripura, South Tripura, North Tripura. The total area of the state is 10491.69 sq. km. According to the Survey of India the total population of Tripura is 31,99,203 as per 2001 census. Out of the total population of Tripura 9,93,426 persons are tribals as per 2001 census.

The origin of the name of Tripura is a highly debated issue. According to "Raj Mala" (literally meaning the garland of kings), Tripura was once ruled by a king named Tripur after whom the state has been named. Another opinion is that, the name Tripura originated from the two words "twi" means water and "pra" means tributary. Together it conveys the meaning of Tripura as a land adjoining the water from different tributaries. This version seems to be relevant and correct as the hill people of Tripura called the state as "Twipra" and not Tripura.

The origin and history of Tripura can be best understood from the "Raj Mala", the chronicles of Tripura. It should be noted that Tripura is only the ruling dynasty that has an era of its own. It dates from 590 A.D. when Raja Birraj extended his conquests beyond the Ganges. According to "Raj Mala", believed to be the oldest book dealing with the history of Tripura nearly 184 Tripuri kings have ruled over the state "Twipra".

The nineteenth century marked the beginning of the modern era in Tripura when king Maharaja Bir Chandra Manikya Bahadur modelled his administrative set up on the British East India Company pattern and brought in some reforms. Maharaja Bir Bikram Kishore Manikya was the last ruler among 184 rajas who ruled over Tripura till 1947. Even during the British rule, Tripura was an administrative princely State. Under the Maharaja, Tripura merged with the Indian Union on October 15, 1949 as a "C" category state.

Agriculture and jhum cultivation is the main source of livelihood. Three-fourth people of the rural areas are directly or indirectly related to the agriculture. So agricultural and jhum produce is the main livelihood of the people of rural tribal areas in Tripura. It is because, the tribal people, mostly reside in the hilly and remote areas. They converted forest lands into agricultural field by clearing forests and making there habitable and, in course of time, we pushed them back again into deeper forests.

Table 4.1

Area and Location of Tripura, 2004-05 Census

1.	Total area (in sq. km)	10,491.69
2.	Altitude at Agartala (in mtr.)	12.80
3.	North latitude	22°56′ & 24°32′
4.	East longitude	91°09′ & 92°20′

5.	Extreme length (in km)	183.5
6.	Extreme width (in km)	112.7
7.	Border with Bangladesh (in km)	856
8.	Border with Mizoram (in km)	109
9.	Border with Assam (in km)	53

Source: Directorate of Economics and Statistics, Govt. of Tripura.

Table 4.1 shows the Geographical area and location of the State Tripura. It has international boundary with Bangladesh of about 856 km, which constitutes nearly 84% of the total perimeter of the state.

Physical Features

Tripura's topography is characterised by hills and plains. The proportional distribution of land between hills and plains is 2:1. There are six major hill ranges covered by evergreen and deciduous forest. From east to west there ranges are Jampui, Sakhntang, Longtherai, Atharamura, Sardang and Barmura. These hill ranges contain several peaks which stands out prominently above the general landscape. The most important of them are—Betlingsib (Jampui Range), Sairunmura, Deotamura, Baramura, Jarimura, Atharamura, Feingpui, Sinbari (Longtherai range) and Sakham (Sakhantang). Betlingsib is the highest peak of Tripura in Jampui range with the height of 979 metres above sea level. The climatic condition of Tripura is shown in table 3.2.

There are eleven rivers in Tripura which have all the characteristics of hill streams. Burima, Dhalai, Deo, Gumti, Haora, Juri, Khowai, Muhuri, Manu and Fenny are the principal rivers of Tripura. The river Gumti is the longest river of the state with a total length of about 176 km. It is formed by the confluence of two smaller rivers—the Raima and the Saima. The Dumbor fall, a spectacular cascading fall has been formed in its course.

The state enjoys a tropical monsoon climate which is very hot and humid. Tripura receives 200-255 cm of rainfall annually. The climate remains fairly dry between October and February.

The state is covered with a variety of soils. Loamy and sandy alluvial soils occupy the river valleys and plains. The red and yellow soils are mostly found along the tillas and are different in organic matter and plant nutrients.

Being in a high rainfall area, the hill contains valuable timber like *sal, jaral, shegun* etc. but mostly they are covered with bamboos and canes.

Table 4.2

Climate in Tripura at a glance (2004) Census

1	Maximum Temperature (May)	37.0 celsius
2	Minimum Temerature (Jan &Dec.)	06.7 celsius
3	Average annual rainfall	254.3 cm
4	Highest rainfall(Kanchanpur)	294.7 cm
5	Total rainy days	99.6

Source: Directorate Economics and Statistics, Govt. of Tripura, Agartala.

The Changing Demography

The state of Tripura is the permanent member of Scheduled tribes besides a large population of the non-tribals. The scheduled castes and scheduled tribes occupy 16.36% and 30.95% of the population of Tripura respectively.

Tripura had been mainly a tribal region even in the recent past when the tribal population predominated; but with the passing of time and growing cultural contacts the nos. of non tribal people who outnumbered the population of the tribal people. In 1931 the total tribal population of Tripura was 52% of the total population of the state where as in 1981 it came down to 28.44%. Tripura is the only state in India where continuous migration from neighbouring Bangladesh have totally upset the local demographic balance and reduced its original tribal inhabitants to a pitiful minority own land.

The growth the population in Tripura and percentage of decadal variation in population is shown in Table 4.3. It shows how the non tribals outnumbered the tribal population in the state over the preceding decades. The decade of merger of Tripura with the Indian Union the population registered an abnormally high growth rate of 78.71% as reflected in 1961 census.

Table 4.3
Tripura's Demographic Change: 1901-2001

Year	*Total Population*	*Percentage variation*	*Tribal Population*	*Percentage of tribal Population to total Population*
1901	1,73,325	25.99	91,678	52.89
1911	2,29,613	32.48	1,11,303	48.47
1921	3,04,347	32.59	1,71,610	56.37
1931	3,82,450	25.63	2,03,327	52.00
1941	5,13,010	34.14	2,56,991	50.09
1951	6,39,028	24.56	2,37,953	37.23
1961	11,42,005	78.71	3,60,070	31.50
1971	15,56,324	36.28	4,50,544	28.95
1981	20,53,058	31.92	5,83,920	28.44
1991	27,57,205	34.30	8,53,345	30.95
2001	31,99,203	16.20	9,9,3,426	31.05

Source: W.W Hunter, pp 484; S. Deb Barma, Census Bibarani 1931; Census of India 1991, 2001.

Table 4.4: Variation of Population, Decadal Growth Rate (in %), Sex Ratio (m/f), Density of Population (Persons per sq. km), Literacy Rate of Tripura's Population (1951-2001)

Year	*Population*	*Decadal Growth Rate (%)*	*Sex Ratio (M/F)*	*Density of Population*	*Literacy Rate (in %)*	*Variation (absolute) (M/F)*	*Literacy Rate*	
1951	6,45,707	+25.87	904	62	15.50	132697	11.8	3.7
1961	11,42,005	+76.86	932	109	20.24	496298	35.3	12.3
1971	15,56,342	+34.28	943	148	30.98	414337	46.8	27.8
1981	20,53,058	+31.92	946	196	42.12	496716	61.5	38.0
1991	27,57,205	+34.30	945	263	60.44	704147	70.0	50.0
2001	31,99,203	+15.74	948	305	73.20	433796	81.0	64.9

Source: Census of India, 1951-2001.

Tribes of Tripura

Speaking about the hill people, particularly the Tripuris, the political Agent wrote in 1873: "The people were very simple, truthful, and honest until corrupted by the evil influence arising from closer intercourse with the inhabitants of the plains, and also by bad government, whereby they were left at the mercy of grasping subordinates. Every advantage was taken of their ignorance and credulity, till meet deceit with its own weapons" (Hunter, pp.438). According to the 1961 census of India, the following Nineteen Scheduled tribes reside in Tripura:

1. Bhil 2. Bhatia 3. Chaimal 4. Chakma 5. Garo 6. Halam 7. Jamatia 8. Khasi 9. Kuki 10. Lepcha 11. Lushai 12. Mog 13. Munda 14. Noatia 15. Orang 16. Reang 17. Santal 18. Tripuri and 19. Uchoi

An interesting point to be noted here is that out of the total nineteen listed scheduled tribes of Tripura only eight tribes, Chaimal, Halam, Jamatia, Kuki, Noatia, Reang, Tripuri and Uchoi; are the local tribes of Tripura. Other tribes like Bhil, Munda, Orang and Santal have come from central Indian tribes; Bhutias and Lepchas have hailed from the northern frontier tribes (Bhutan, Sikkim and north Bengal); Garo, Khasi, and Lushai are said to be from the neighbouring state of Meghalaya; and the Chakmas and the Mogs have come from Chittagong hill tracts and the Arakans.

The break-up of the tribal population into different individual tribes is given in Table 4.5.

It is evident from the given table as shown that Tripuris constitute the largest tribal group followed by the Reangs in Tripura. According to the 2001 census, out of the total tribal population, 993426 persons, these two largest tribal group in Tripura captured 54.47% and 16.62% respectively.

Hence, it is important to note that the census has identified some unspecified tribal groups with a population of 7098 persons as per the 2001 census.

Table 4.5: Tribe Wise Population of Tripura at a Glance (1951-2001) Census

Name of Tribe	*1951*	*1961*	*1971*	*1981*	*1991*	*2001*
1. Bhil	41	69	169	898	1754	2336
2. Bhutia	19	7	3	22	47	29
3. Chaimal	220	50		18	26	226
4. Chakma	7277	22386	28662	34797	96096	64293
5. Garo	7352	5484	5559	7297	96096	64293
6. Halam	1644	16296	19076	28969	36499	47245
7. Jamatia	2764	24359	34192	44501	60824	74949
8. Khasi	151	349	491	457	358	630
9. Kuki	2721	5531	7775	5501	10628	11674
10. Lepcha	5	7	14	106	111	105
11. Mog	3789	10524	13273	181231	31612	30385
12. Munda, Kaur	51	4409	5347	7993	11547	12416
14. Noatia	1916	16010	10297	7182	4158	6655
15. Orang		2875	3428	5271	6751	6223
16. Reang	8471	56597	64722	84003	11606	165103
17. Santal	736	1562	2222	2726	2736	2151
18. Tripuri	150971	189799	250545	330872	461531	543848
19. Uchoi	-	766	1061	1306	1637	2103
Unspecified	2218	-	36	-	-	7098
Total	192293	360070	450544	583700	853345	993426

Source: Census of India, Tripura, 1951, 1961, 1971, 1981, 1991, 2001.

All these tribes practised shifting cultivation to produce food grains, vegetable, cotton, sesame (oil seed) etc. They collected forest products freely for meeting their innumerable needs. They reared poultry and pig and also collect meat by hunting wild animals. They also practised the art of weaving which is very common in the tribal society of Tripura. In keeping with the egalitarian ethos simple social security measures were taken by them.

5

Results

In this section, Rural Institutions in the Block are viewed in broad sense through Economic Sectors and Social Sectors. As agriculture still remains the main economic base for the rural population, agricultural development has only been taken to describe economic sector in this study. On the contrary, Social Sectors comprise of a number of developmental variables namely: Education, Health and Sanitation, Transport and Communications, Other Institutions (which include market, grocery shop, electricity, PDS, well, bio-gas and library), Financial Institutions (consisting of Non-institutional as well as Institutional rural credit structures) and Rural Development Institutions (like SHGs, panchayat, club, ICDS centre, BL&LRO and Block Office). These entire broad seven "Sectors", as a whole, reflects the extent of Social development in the block.

The few of those like SHGs, SSA, Primary school, Health Centre, Panchayat etc., have been taken for in-depth study and to find out the role of rural institutions for rural empowerment

Education directs the standard of employment. Health & Nutrition depend on Education & income. Ability to work depends on good physique. Communication gives the opportunity of education & employment as well. The concept of Global Village emanates from a sound communication system world wide. The other Institutions like Financial Institutions and Rural Development Institution affect the Economic Sector as well as Social Sectors as a whole. All these sectors are thus interrelated with each another.

SHG as an Institution

The Govt. of India has started SGSY as a major Self-employment Programme since April 1999. It is a holistic programme with an objective to bring poor families above poverty line. Under SGSY, poor families are organized into SHG through the process of social mobilization. This programme ensures training and capacity building and provides income generation assistance through bank credits and Govt. subsidies. Under the scheme, financial assistance is given to SHGs belonging to BPL families.

Self-help Group is a voluntary group formed to attain common goal and provide self-sufficiency and moral support including monetary aid to each other among the groups in times of difficulties.

Conceptually, SHG is a homogenous group formed to earn mutually and agree to contribute to the common fund from which the members will be given or lent for productive and emergent credit needs. The concept of SHG evolved form women organization from women voluntary organization during 1990s. SHGs are motivated to function as an element of social change, gender awareness, social education, training and improved human resource.

The SHGs usually target the grass root people to increase their knowledge and skills as well as elevation in decision making power.

Since independence, the Planning Commission with an aim to converge benefit and socio-economic development especially for women, the "9th plan envisaged inclusion of an identifiable woman component plan in the programmes of respective ministries right from the planning process, monitoring and implementation of programmes to ensure benefit of women". The 9th plan document 1997-2002 laid emphasis on participation of people in the planning process and promotion of SHGs. Empowerment of women was one of the primary objectives of the 9th plan.

Programme of self-employment has been an important component of anti-poverty programmes implemented through Govt. initiatives in rural India. The emergence of SHG was a post plan after the failure of many big schemes to aid the poor and marginalized people of rural India.

SHG is one of the greatest self-help aid which acts both as voluntary and as a unit. Under SGSY, though it was started, today it has gained immense prestige and faith and trust among the rural Indian people. In the year 2005, the 10th Five Year Plan gave much emphasis on women empowerment and child development. It is believed that existence of SHGs will not only improve the economic condition of women but also will improve their decision making skills.

Self-help group is a common stand by every individual member of the group. They are also known as solidarity group since they provide moral support to each other and their common fund help individual group members in times of need.

However, the 9th Five Year Plan document recognizes that inspite of developmental measures and constitutional legal guarantees; women have lagged behind in almost all sectors. Though the Govt. has continued to allocate resource and formulated policies for the empowerment of women, it has become strikingly clear that political and social forces resist women rights in the name of religion, culture or ethnic tradition to marginalize an oppression of women.

The basic issue that prevents women from playing full participatory role in the nation building is a lack of economic independence. Self-help groups have been considered as one of the most significant tool to achieve desired goals.

Characteristics of SHG

The basic objective of SHG is that it acts as the forum for members to provide space and support to each other. SHG comprises of very poor people who do not have access to formal financial institution. It enables its members to learn to cooperate and work in a group environment. An SHG is group of people that meets regularly to discuss issues of interest and to look at solutions of commonly experienced problems.

The group may or may not be promoted by Govt. or non-Government institutions. SHG is always considered as an important institution for improving the life of women in various economic and social components such as health, education, sanitation, child care, human rights etc. However in reality, it does not happen without any specific inputs or direction.

Identification of Beneficiaries

For the purpose of awareness building regarding benefits of entrepreneurship and self-help groups, an information was conducted though public meeting, brochures, posters, visual- aids and skits. Thus, it was realized that selection of :nembers should convey certain requirements.

Formation of SHGs

- Number of members must be from 5 to 15.
- Not more than 1 member from a single household.
- Criteria and procedure for approving individual members or loan applications.
- Regular attendance at the meetings.

Table 5.1: SHGs in Different Districts

Sl. No.	*Item*	*Dhalai*	*South*	*North*	*West*	*Total*
1.	SHG formed 2005-06	640	1000	800	1560	4000
2.	ST	136	111	85	135	467
3.	SC	46	85	59	73	263
4.	Rural minorities	-	20	49	20	89
5.	OBC	21	65	50	44	180
6.	Others	29	43	65	93	230
7.	Women	109	231	161	290	791
8.	PH	Nil	4	Nil	Nil	4
9.	SHG 1st grade completion during the year	181	376	334	218	1109

10.	Revolving fund paid to SHG during the year	96	373	336	610	1415
11.	CC account opened by SHG during the year	123	291	168	712	1294
12.	SHG 2nd grade completion	231	415	292	667	1605
13.	Groups sponsored for bank loans during the year	110	128	82	727	1047
14.	Group received bank loan during the year	51	95	3	121	270
	ST	17	24	1	37	79
	SC	15	27	Nil	18	60
	Rural minorities	1	Nil	Nil	5	6
	OBC	12	18	Nil	3	33
	Others	6	26	2	58	92
	Women	21	66	1	60	148
	PH	1	-	-	-	1
15.	Credit dispersed to group during the year	87.05	171.27	84.29	46.00	808.61

Objectives

- Savings/Thrift
- Internal, external and inter lending.
- Social development oriented.
- Discussion on common problems.
- Income generation and gradually becoming self-reliant.

SHG in Tripura

SGSY was launched in 1st April 1999 all over India as a convergence of Integrated Rural Development Programme (IRDP), Training of Rural Youth in Self-employment (TRYSEM), supply of improved tool kits to rural artisans and many more other developmental schemes.

The primary objective of the scheme was to alleviate the BPL families and give priority to women empowerment through the formation of SHG. Below is given some of the distribution of SHG formation in the four districts of Tripura.

Positives of SHG

The SHG in Tripura came with a holistic approach and still is persistent in its ideal characters. Since the formation of SHG in every rural village of the 4 districts in Tripura, the women especially have been in the advantageous position. Constant link with the facilitator, Govt. officials, banks and other organizations gave the women an exposure regarding the latest schemes, policies and realization of their needs. The DRDA is playing an active role in cultivating these activities with full acceleration. SHG aims at providing awareness among rural residents regarding sanitation, water, civic life, self-employment, entrepreneurial activity, health, child care, educational upliftment etc.

Since human resource plays an active role in increasing GNP and maintaining sustainable development and women are part of the society. As such, development of female human resource will be a pivotal part of developmental tool. SHG maximizes certain elements in human and society that affects the fusion of societal development such as,

- Increasing self-confidence.
- Promotion of entrepreneurial activity.
- Alleviating weaker sections of the society.
- Increase employment possibilities.
- Enhance position of savings.
- Prompt team work among the members.
- Solve problems with joint endeavor.
- Cultivate empowerment of women.

Citing the vast potential of SHG, institutions and voluntary organizations and NABARD has recognized SHGs, though unregistered. Several rural branches of nationalized and commercial banks have come up to aid SHG. Due to it, SHGs has become an effective approach to outreach the poor rural women under poverty alleviation programme.

Approaches for Poverty Alleviation through SHGs in Tripura

In Tripura, initiatives have been taken in the formation of SHGs through out the state. This may be categorized in the three main broad points according to their involvement as primary groups.

1. Initiatives taken by Government
2. Initiatives taken by NABARD
3. Initiatives taken by voluntary organization.

Initiatives Taken by Government

Government departments like the DRDA, Tribal re habilitation implantation and primitive Group Programme, Fishery department, Social welfare department, Education department, SC & OBC Welfare department, Rural development department, Handloom and Handicraft, Agriculture and horticulture department etc and many as such has contributed in the assistance of alleviating the rural people through SHGs.

Among them the department of Rural Development has launched the SGSY as he most effective programme, which targets at grass root level people. It is the soul target of SGSY to incorporate self-sufficiency in among the rural peoples of India especially among the ST, SC peoples and OBCs. Keeping in mind thus SHGs were formed for the active participation of men and women and their opinion in the planning process.

Eventually in the area of Jampuijala block, the compositions of families are basically of, father and mother and his one or several son and their daughter in law. All the families are mostly joint or semi-joint family type.

Table 5.2: Family Type

Family Type	*Number*	*Percentage*
Joint	17	56. 67
Nuclear	13	43.33

Source: Field survey.

During the study the result came up as, out of thirty members seventeen of them had joint family and only thirteen of them had nuclear families. Though there is not much difference in the distribution of family types yet it was quite hard to distinguish a perfect nuclear family.

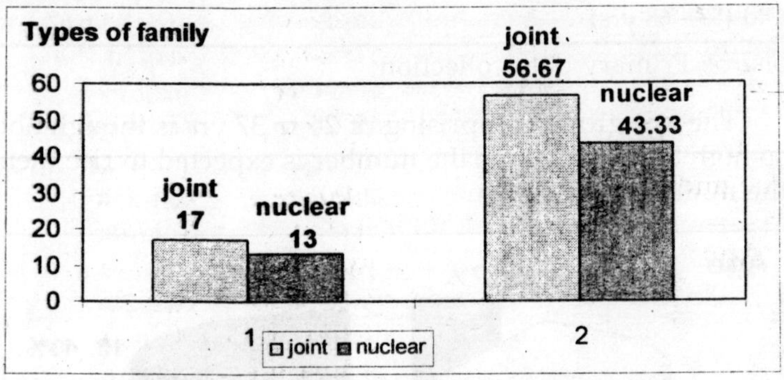

The graphical presentation shows that 56.67 percent consist of joint family where as only 43.33 percent consist of only nuclear family. But it must be mentioned here that out pf this nuclear family very few were perfectly nuclear in nature and one or two had perfectly joint family character. There joint family types may indicate the disguised employment possibilities. The nuclear type, lack of manpower and effective income, this perhaps led to joining of SHGs with a view to develop themselves.

Age composition

It is quite interesting to observe that most of the SHG members are of middle age and they are intend to earn a good living and come to their solution of societal problem. The age group is from 24 yrs to 45 yrs. It is to be noticed that most of the members are within the age of 45 yrs, and they are quite in number.

Table 5.3: Age Composition of Sample Households

Age	*Number*	*Percentage*
Young (24 - 37 yrs)	13	43.33
Middle (38 - 52 yrs)	14	46.67
Old (53 - 68 yrs)	2	6.67

Source: Primary data collection.

The age group comprising of 24 to 37 yrs is though not so high but in due time the number is expected to rise then the middle age women.

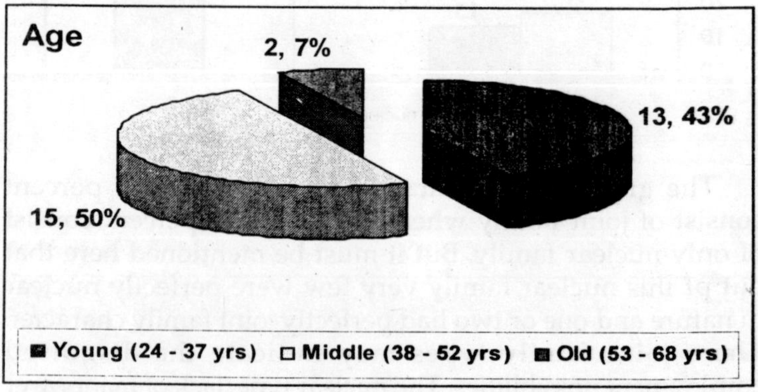

That of middle age members has experienced the various constraints of life and lastly they have formed the group in order to gain a social benefit through any economic activity, and that became possible only through SHG formation.

Residence Quality

Most of the members live in traditional types of houses made up of bamboo, hay, mud with the roof made up of tin or wild hay. As a matter of fact the entire house system is traditional as such the residence quality must not mean they cannot change their living standard or they cannot afford to choose one. How ever there are some of the members who are really poor and absolutely below poverty line.

Table 5.4

House Condition of the Sample Households

Type of house	*Number*	*Percentage*
Hut	7	23.33
Katcha	5	16. 67
Pucca	3	10
Mixed	8	26. 67
Others	2	6. 67

Source: Primary data collection.

As the study is mainly on women consequently all members belonged to tribal community and they live in types of houses where change is absolute and consistent due to earning possibility.

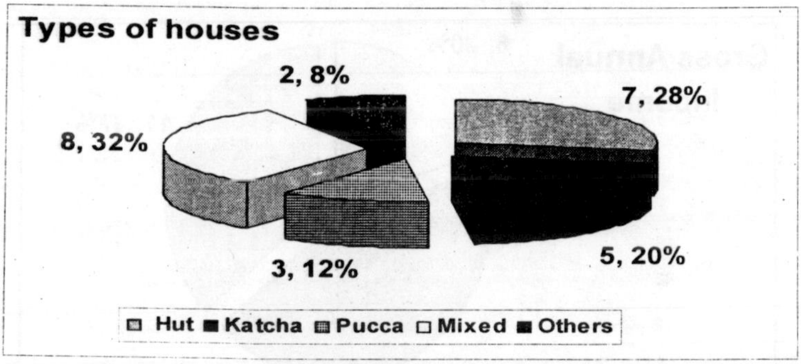

Mixed types of houses are greater in number to 8.32 percent, where the hut houses are of 7.28 percent, and others 5.20 katcha, 3.12 pucca and 2.8 percent comprises of good house holds. Like the pucca, this is based on concrete structure. It may be of mud but the structure is better and organized. Thus it indicates that the living standards of people are moderate in terms of houses.

Income

Almost all the members are related with entrepreneurial activity especially in the livestock business. All the SHG groups are quite self sufficient in terms of business. As we can see their annual income is averagely higher. There are 13 groups which earn thirty thousand and above per annum only by selling stocks. However there are small earners too below 10 thousand per annum.

Table 5.5: Gross Annual Income

Gross annual income	*Number*	*Percentage*
Low (<10,000)	11	36.67
Middle (10,000 - 30,000)	13	43.33
High (>30,000)	6	20.00

Source: Primary data collection.

The graphical presentation of the annual income clearly indicates the average income will be higher then the low income group. However the time will be the perfect story teller regarding the social development and the achievement.

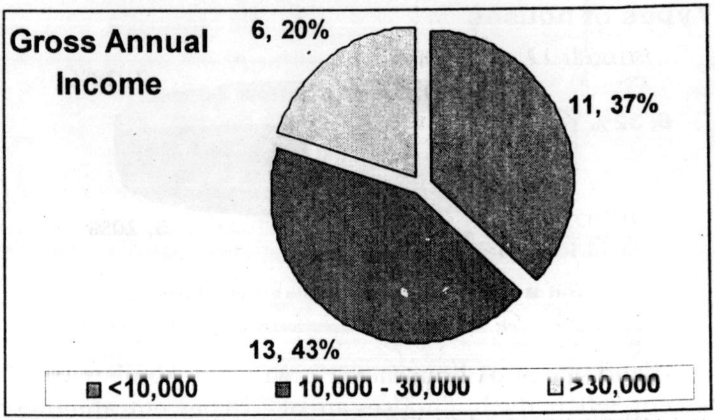

When we talk about the SHG members we must know that most of the members belong to BPL category. The money they contribute as fund in the group is very meager as such keeping that in mind there income must be very promising. Thus it also indicates the alleviation in living standard due to positive earning.

Good flow of income truly reflects the way of living in the rural areas. The following table and chart is clearly indicating that there is some positive sign in this respect.

Table 5.6: Availability of Luxurious Goods

Availability of luxurious goods	*Number*	*Percentage*
T.V. 7	23.33	
Radio 17	56.67	
Fan 27	90.00	
Motor cycle	2	6.67
Cycle 12	40.00	
Others 6	20.00	

Source: Primary data collection.

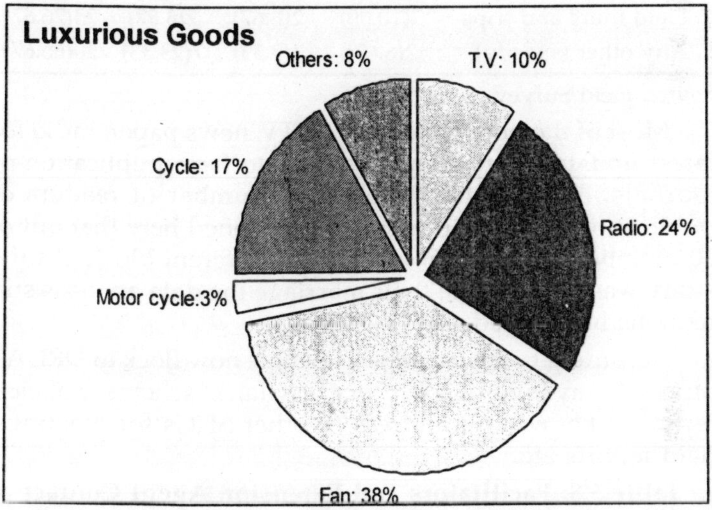

Surprisingly most of the houses have television, radio, fan etc. The majority of the houses has fan, either ceiling or the table fan. The members also prefer hearing radios, so most of the houses have radio too. As in rural places radio can only be the means of communication and knowledge and entertainment. However the TV has taken the place of radio.

In the above pie diagram the distribution of luxurious goods surely indicates the awareness of the Group members and there intentions towards the goal. Beside the people prefer to be liberal in case of needs and conscious about requirements of their basic amenities. It will be clearer from the next diagram.

This statistical presentation indicates the true nature of their consciousness regarding their action and intension towards their goal.

Table 5.7: Mass Media Exposer

Mass media exposure	*Most often*	*Often*	*Rarely*	*Never*
1. Newspaper	13(43.33)	3(10)	0	14(46.67)
2. Television	14(40.00)	4(13.33)	2(6.67)	10(33.33)
3. Radio	12(33.33)	5(16.67)	1(3.33)	12(40)
4. Farm publication	10(33.33)	6(20)	1(3.33)	13(43.33)
5. Field tours and trips	3(10.00)	2(6.67)	2(6.67)	23(76.67)
6. Any other (specify)	2(6.67)	1(3.33)	7(23.33)	20(66.67)

Source: Field Survey.

Most of the people depend on TV, news paper, radio for latest updates. Very few have gone to farm publication or journals. But the chart shows the number of readers of publication is ten, so it must be mentioned here that out of 10 members 8 has been married to different block. As the study was done before their marriage the data analysis still remains unchanged.

According to the latest news people now flock to DRDA's office for any kind of assistance, say latest scheme, policies, technical know how, address of other SHGs for meetings, field reports etc.

Table 5.8: Facilitators and Extension Agent Contact

Extension Agent Contact	*Most Often*	*%*	*Often (N)*	*%*	*Rarely (N)*	*%*	*Never (N)*	*%*
Veterinary officers/ Govt officials	2	6.67	3	10	17	56.67	8	26.67
Scientists	0	0.00	0	0	1	3.33	29	96.67
Extension agents/ personnel's	14	46.67	10	33.33	6	20.00	0	0.00
Block officials	7	23.33	6	20.00	12	40.00	5	16.67
Panchayat personnel	17	56.67	11	36.67	2	6.67	0	0.00
Vety field assistant/ stockmen	2	6.67	9	30.00	12	40.00	7	23.33

Bank personnel	23	76.67	7	23.33	0	0.00	0	0.00
N.G.O	20	66.67	6	20.00	4	13.33	0	0.00
Other S.H.G's	24	80.00	6	20.00	0	0.00	0	0.00
Family members	18	60.00	10	33.33	2	6.67	0	0.00

Source: Primary data collection.

On the above chart it indicates that most of the members often meet the Banks for loans and other financial assistance, Panchayat for the governmental policies and programmes, veterinary doctors in relation to their livestock concern.

Most rarely the meet or never meet are the scientist of agriculture department or any government officials. On being asked the reason behind it they say the officials ignore them and most of them cannot speak the regional language *kokborok,* as they are non-tribal.

Consciousness regarding the health is very high among the members. It was noticed that most of them possessive about their child's health and is ready to give full attention, as such the percentage of ranking is higher in concerned to children's. Women generally care much about their family and very less about themselves. Rather they are much concerned about other members of their SHG.

Table 5.9: Health Awareness

Health awareness	*Number*	*Percentage*	*Rank*
Self	4	13.33	4
Child	30	100.00	1
Family	26	86.67	2
Others	7	23.33	3

Source: Primary data collection

The graphical presentation is merely representing the percentage of their concern towards their health consciousness.

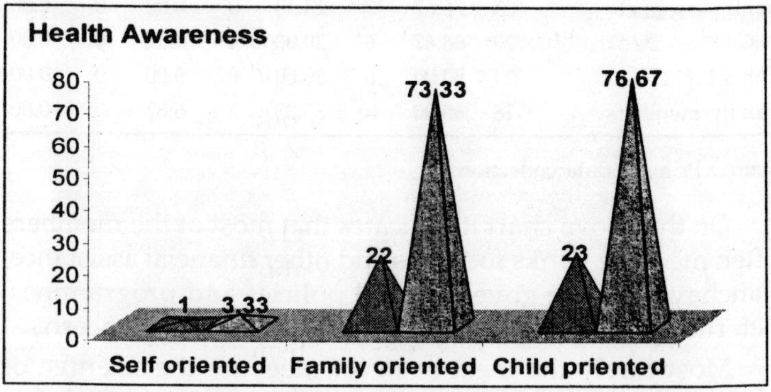

In this chart it clearly shows that most of the decision regarding the education is majorly taken by the female members. Thus it proves that they are much more wise decision taker than the male members of the family.

Table 5.10: Family Decisions

Family decision	*Female's Participation (Number)*	*Percentage (%)*
Regarding education	28	93.33
Regarding health	26	86.67
Regarding monitory matters	7	23.33

Source: Primary data collection.

Health related decision is taken by the women too, thus it indicates the growing power of women in decision making process, especially in family. When a woman takes a decision specially regarding the family they are always the wisest and reliable as it is them who are managing the family and it is them who understands the problem better.

Majority of the group are engaged in livestock activity, which is a good sign because the livestock business gives a outcome in shorter period of time. The members are in option to choose any of the entrepreneurial activity, but they rather choose livestock as they are aware that this farming has shorter duration of outcome.

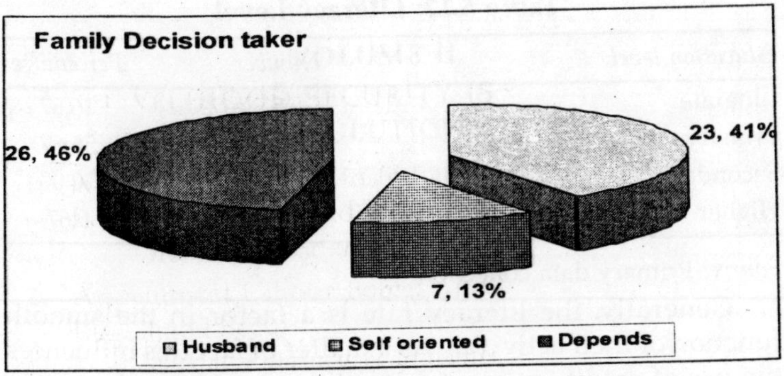

Table 5.11: Economic Activity

Economic activities	*Number*	*Percentage*
Livestock	17	56.67
SSI	2	6.67
Cottage industries	9	30.00
Others	2	6.67
Nothing	0	0.00

Source: Primary data collection.

Besides the cottage industry too has a great output which is evident from the number of members involved in it. This type of work basically includes Rignai making, a traditional garment of the tribal, than statues made up of bamboo, etc.

Two members group are engaged in small scale industries and other two are in pisci culture and banana plantation. Among the livestock business the groups carried the piggery and gottary farming.

On the basis of study conducted on the sample it was found that all the members who made groups were more or less literate. But the sad news is according to government criteria any individual who can write names are termed as literate as such they too are regarded as literate. But on practical ground the members often cannot cop up or understand the official languages owing to which they face problems in carrying out their works in relation to their SHG.

Table 5.12: Literacy Level

Education level	*Number*	*Percentage*
Illiterate	5	16.67
Primary	17	56.67
Secondary	6	20.00
Higher	2	6.67

Source: Primary data collection.

Generally, the literacy rate is a factor in the smooth function of their activities. As a matter of fact this influences the use of credit for economic betterment of women. As in the table two members has finished up to +2, and seventeen of them primary, and six of them secondary. This is good sign though, there are many who hardly can read or write.

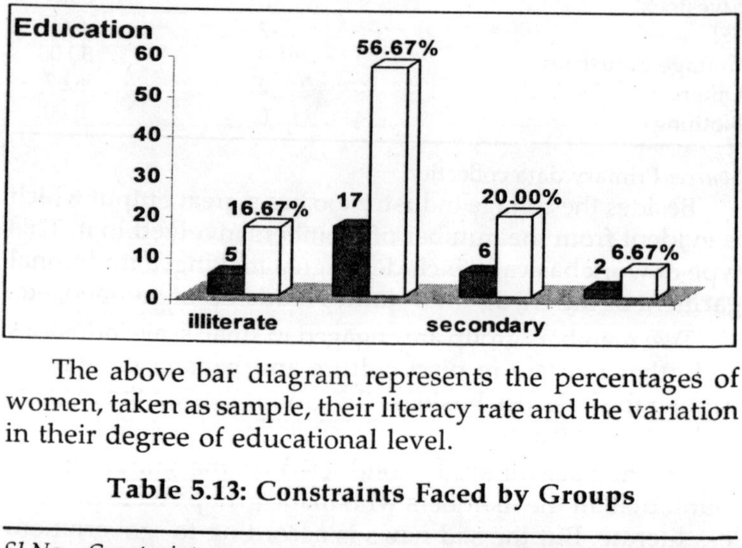

The above bar diagram represents the percentages of women, taken as sample, their literacy rate and the variation in their degree of educational level.

Table 5.13: Constraints Faced by Groups

Sl.No.	*Constraint*	*Number (Yes)*	*%*	*Rank*
1.	Economic constraint	24	80.00	2
2.	Lack of infrastructure facility	30	100.00	1
3.	Distant marketing place	21	70.00	3
4.	Non availability of Govt. schemes for smooth functioning	17	56.67	4
5.	Lack of good market value	10	33.33	5

	for revenue generation			
6.	Low availability of family labour	7	23.33	6
7.	Others/ specify	0	0	-

Source: Primary data collection.

Some of the major drawbacks faced by all the groups are the capital problem or the allocation of fund to run the business. The governmental facility is not penetrating enough to facilitate the people. There is a major problem of communication with the market of the urban areas such as Takarjala to Agartala, Gabordip to Agartala, Pekuwajola to Agartala, etc.

Beside there is no effective governmental scheme to undertake some initiatives in an affective manner to develop the economic condition of the SHGs. As such the producers has to sell there goods in local market getting minimum profit.

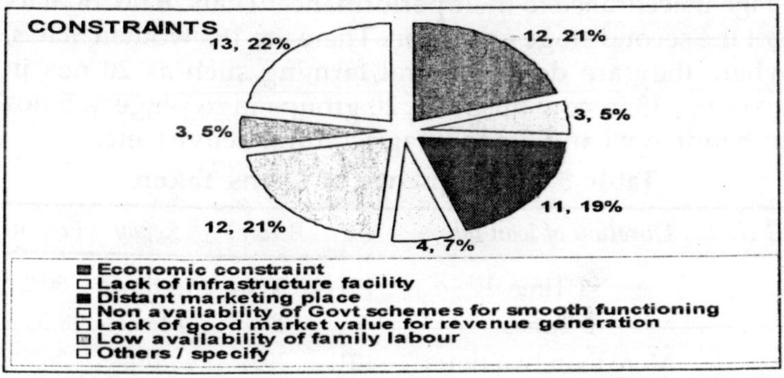

Some time the governmental officials remain absent in the office due to life threat and no availability of transportation. Besides the motivator village level worker, panchayat officials are not effective in the field work.

Financial Institutions

1. State Bank of India
2. Gramin Bank
3. Governmental Institutions like DRDA, Agri. Dept., etc.

4. Other Financial institution NGOs, VOs, Cooperative Bank etc.

There was state bank earlier but the branch was transferred to Gulaghati, due to Insurgency problem. There was Gramin bank earlier but it is closed now, there is no other institution to provide with financial assistance.

In case of governmental institution the DRDA, the Animal husbandry department provide with all necessary support and financial assistance. SGSY financed to 26 SHGs for the entrepreneurial activity.

The NGOs, VOs provide financial assistance along with technical know how like training, adult education, awareness generation on health and hygiene etc.

SHG Gradation

Out of 301 ST SHGs 70 of them got the gradation of first stage inaccordace to their performance. Than 26 no. of SHG got the second stage gradation. There are 190 women SHGs, where they are doing several farming such as 20 nos in goattary, 13 in cow business, 20 groups in to piggery, 5 nos in handlooms and 7 nos in agricultural activity etc.

Table 5.14: Frequency of Loans Taken

Sl No	*Duration of loan taken*	*Nos*	*Percent*	*Repay*	*Percent*
1.	1 Time	15	50%	15 times	50%
2.	2 Times	5	20%	4 times	18.50%
3.	More than two times	10	30%	10 times	30%

Source: Primary data collection.

The SHG members has taken loans on various grounds some times due to health related problems and some time due to other social problems such as paying fees for children's school, then for purchasing of fodder for their cattle. Here one thing was to be noticed that all the members who has taken loans has returned them with interest in time.

Social Mobilization

'Social mobilisation' is commonly considered to be an

important dimension of capacity-, and institution-building, particularly when relating to disadvantaged people.

Social mobilisation may occur at all levels. Most often, however, the term is used for activities in local communities, although not necessarily confined to such communities. When thus confined, the process is commonly referred to as community mobilization. This may involve whole communities or be limited to sections of communities (for instance, land-less people or groups of particularly poor women).

Women have extensive work loads with dual responsibility for farm and household production. Their work is getting harder and more time-consuming due to ecological degradation and changing agricultural technologies and practices. Women also have an active role and extensive involvement in livestock production, forest resource use and fishery processing and contribute considerably to household income through farm and non-farm activities as well as through work as landless agricultural labourers. However, women's work as family labour is underestimated and there are high degrees of interstate and intra-state variations in gender roles in agriculture, environment and rural production.

The SHGs are working in this area as a social mobiliser through their groups and it is held purely with the help of women members of the groups. Although on an off they take help of their husband or male members of their family to facilitate the whole programme smoothly. It is also noticed that the women members of the SHGs are good facilitators as well as social mobiliser for the social development of their society. The following cases are noticed in the study area:

- SHGs are formed with the help of SHGs
- Collective work is done with the help of women of the SHGs
- Women members work for their child education development
- Groups members help another group to solve any problem
- All SHGs are linked with the other groups and community for their betterment

- Arrange awareness camp on health to rejoice women's day or any important day
- Established link with the different organisations like DRDA, SBI, Line department of Government etc.
- Women's ability are enhanced, their problems and possible solutions are traced by themselves, group and individual skills are augmented with the help of SHGs and the disadvantaged has come forward to take any type of assignment for their development and social development as well

Self-Help Groups and Women's Empowerment

A great deal of evidence from around the world indicates that gender inequalities undermine the effectiveness of development policies. It is seen that despite progress, gender disparities persist around the world. For example, in no region do women and men have equal rights. In a number of countries, women still lack independent access to land, manage property, conduct business, or even travel without their husband's consent;

Women continue to have systematically poorer command over a range of productive resources, including land, information and financial resources.

The government of India has declared the year as Women Empowerment Year. The year 2001 was formally launched by PM in a function held at Vigyan Bhawan on 4th January, 2001, where the Stree Shakti Puruskar was also awarded to five distinguished grass root level women had made outstanding services in the field of social service, education, economic empowerment women in remote and difficult areas.

Despite considerable increases in women's education, relative to men, women continue to have limited opportunities and earn less than men in the labour market even when they have the same education and work experience as men;

Women remain vastly underrepresented in politics and policymaking. They hold less than 10 per cent of the seats in parliament in most regions and less than 8 per cent in government ministerial positions (King & Mason, 2001).

As pointed out by the recent report (Sen & Kumar, 2001) commissioned by the office of the United Nations Resident Coordinator in India, women in India:

- Are outnumbered by men-there are an estimated 39 million missing women;
- Face nutritional discrimination;
- Have little control over own fertility and reproductive health;
- Are less literate with higher dropout rates;

Women also provide bulk of the labour in rice cultivation, and, in the plantation sector also, women are the crucial labourers. Depending on the region and crops, women's contributions vary, but they provide labour from planting to harvesting and post-harvest operations. In general, it is understood that women in tribal households, enjoy more decision-making power than women in many other Indian households because of their greater contribution to household income..

Sharp decline in common/ real estate property land on one hand and the deterioration of the remaining land have jointly contributed to hardship for the rural community, particularly for women of the poor households

It is seen that gender Inequality retards economic growth. There is growing evidence to suggest that several aspects of gender relations, the gender-based division of labour, disparities between males and females in power and resources, and gender biases in rights and entitlements-act to undermine economic growth and reduce the well being of men, women and children. It is commonly held that, investments in female education and health tend to increase the incomes of families; educated women who know more about health and hygiene, are also able to practice this knowledge; better educated women are able to adapt newer technologies, hold on to new opportunities, and cope with economic shocks. It is also seen that, early childbearing and frequent pregnancies can interrupt women's education, limit their ability to engage in income generation and force girl children to drop out to take care of the siblings. Women, especially the poor, work longer than men. This limits their participation in income generation activities or community decision making. In addition, women have poorer command over productive resources like education, land, information and financial resources, exercise limited decision-making power and have insignificant political influence as compared to men.

Women's development has come a long way from the earlier welfare orientation. In the welfarist approach, women were taken as vulnerable sections of the population, whose situation could be ameliorated through the provision of support services like health, nutrition and child care. Women's development has been looked at variously from perspectives that have followed the welfare approach. For example, the economic self-reliance puts emphasis on income generation projects for women; the equality model put the blame on inequality and promoted affirmative action to promote equal opportunity. The present approaches of empowerment looks at unequal gender and power relations and uses conscientisation, mobilization, solidarity and collective action as the solutions.

Gender needs developed on the work of Caroline Moser can be useful in planning "empowerment interventions" for the members of the SHG. This concept recognizes women as active partners in development. It also recognizes that women do not participate in development on equal terms with men because of their subordinate position. There is thus, need to classify planning interventions in terms of those that meet practical gender needs-that is, the needs identified to help women in their existing subordinate position in society- and strategic gender needs, namely the needs identified to transform existing subordinate relationships between men and women.

On the other hand, strategic gender needs are those needs that women identify because of their subordinate position in society. They arise from their disadvantaged position in society. They vary according to particular contexts, related to gender divisions of labour, power and control, and may include such issues as legal rights, domestic violence, equal wages, and women's control over their bodies.

Strategic interests are sometimes vague and difficult for women to identify. Even when women know options for change, practical needs and family survival are the first priorities. Women need to be given the opportunity to be able to describe their situation, condition and position. Strategic needs emerge in women's gatherings and in informal consciousness raising processes

Some of the strategic needs and interests of women as a group include:

- Reduced vulnerability to violence and exploitation;
- More economic security, independence, options and opportunities;
- Shared responsibility for reproductive work with men and the state;
- Organising with other women for strength, solidarity and action;
- Increased political power;
- Increased ability to improve the lives and futures of their children; and
- More humanistic and just development processes (ICECD, undated).

As discussed earlier, poverty is multi-dimensional, including material deprivation, low human development, lack of voice and ability to influence decisions that affect lives, and acute vulnerability to adverse shocks. The three critical pillars identified for addressing gender disparities are opportunity, empowerment and security. Some of the interventions that fall under opportunity include the expanding of women's assets, tackling structural inequalities and making markets more responsive to women. Under empowerment, the interventions would be concerned about making institutions work for women, building social capital, removing social barriers, and curbing corruption. Interventions for security would necessitate helping women manage risk, and social protection during crisis.

Empowering women socio-economically through increased awareness of their rights and duties as well as access to resource is a decisive step towards greater security, for them. Women are in new deal today as they are in the focus of economic development. All possible steps are being taken to strengthen them to achieve their economic, social and cultural growth and welfare. The status of women is a barometer of democratism of any state, an indicator of how human right is respected in it.

According to Mikhail Gorvachev "The root cause of women oppression India is the existence of Patriarchy, which has snatched the legitimate right of the women, leaving them completely defenseless and weak."

Today the emerging changes in the values and attitude of the members of SHG are a clear manifestation of socio-economic empowerment interventions yielding relatively quicker result. The socio –economic programmes reinforce each other promote all round development of the children women the house hold the communities etc. It is a process which ultimately leads to self sufficiency and self fulfillment of each member of the society. It is in the direction that SHG are moving towards fulfilling their objectives with meaningful strategic direction.

As per the 1991 Census, the Indian work force participation rate is 37.7 per cent, out of which, the rate for women is 22.7 per cent, which is less than half the rate of 51.6 per cent for men.

During the course of study in this area, a bond developed which gave a clear idea of most un-natural outcome. The government has more than enough scheme for the development of the block, but it is the insurgency problem owing to which the facilitator are not being able to penetrate in the interior of the jampuijala villages. It would be an outrageous act to accuse government for the failure of certain policies and schemes. In this context it can be said that under the DRDA, inspite of less worker the department is facilitating well enough in the upliftment of rural people in this area. The animal husbandry is also facilitating enough in the livestock production of the SHG groups from all dimensions, possible.

The inherent lacuna in the system of function is the mass illiteracy, though few are still on the average rate,

- Absence of active voluntary institutions,

- Voluntary organization for credit disperses,
- Dependence of, on agrarian works,
- Disguised employment, and most ironically
- Unawareness regarding the arrival of existence of new potential schemes made by the government.
- Distressed sell of their product for poor economic condition

Though these may seem very easy and may sound nuisance yet these things are really hampering in the growth of economic development along with the SHGs.

Measures Suggested for the Empowerment of Women

In order to bring women in the centre stage of development and thereby ensuring better participation in the developmental efforts of the nation and enabling them to take a lead role in social and economic development, the following suggestion may be conceded.

Compulsory Education

Eradication of illiteracy of is the first step towards the empowerment of women. Knowledge is power. When a woman is educated the entire family is affected with the goodness of it. Research shows that family with woman of high education or average discards evils like child labour, superstitions, gender discriminations etc. Thus education must be made compulsory in order to empower woman.

Mental Revolution

As William James said "the greatest discovery of any generation is that human being can alter his life by altering his attitude".

As such women must be prompted to participate in active out door works, make differences in their life by being wise and aware of their rights, power, capacity to endure the opportunity and take benefit out of it. They must cherish emotional, intellectual and economic freedom then their counterpart. Emotional maturity and progressive thinking may take them to a life more rewarding and self satisfying.

Credit Facilities

Facilitation in terms of micro credit and liberal supply of credit will go long way in promoting no financial incentives which will go long way in promoting self employment among women through micro enterprise. The appropriate authorities must should provide managerial and marketing facilities whenever where ever necessary. Training and technical consultancy services must be made available close to their station. Adequate supply of information is also essential for their success.

Gainful employment

Women should find appropriate occupation to support them and lead a life contributing to the economic status of her family as well as the nation. Under present condition self employment is the only feasible answer that warrants economic power to the millions of women in the unorganized sector of our economy. Though education is the primary ingredient for empowerment but it is the economic power that acts instantly. Having economic power and occupation of their own would really provide them with many opportunities to prove their potential and moving towards higher levels of achievement.

Account their Views

It should be kept in mind that since it is the policies we are making for them to facilitate them we must include them in the decision making and planning process. Women are not naive it is us who treat hem to be fragile and temper less, so in order to make them empowered we must make sure they are mentally prepared and ready for the action. Their views regarding policies facilitation and other works must be given respect and if necessary implementation.

Health as an Institution

Health, defined as the state of complete physical, mental, social and spiritual well-being and not merely absence of disease and infirmity, proves to be a major contributor to the level of quality of life. The basic objective of human development is to improve the quality of life. Healthy population plays a key role in achieving the development activities as health helps to improve the productivity of mankind both directly and indirectly. The health picture of our country is far from satisfactory. The situation in rural areas of India, where over two thirds of our population lives, in worse position, with only rudimentary health care services being available to the masses all the recent advantages of medical science and technology have not reached the majority of the disadvantaged people living in rural India .Poor socio-economic status and poor health status together make a vicious cycle where in poverty brings in inadequate nutrition, unhealthy environment, sickness causing low productivity and hence poverty. India with a wide range of topographic and climatic conditions has witnessed various types of natural disasters.

It is estimated that 70-75% of all the deaths of children below. 5 years of age in the developing countries is because of three categories of diseases infections spread through human excreta, airborne infections and malnutrition and all of these can very easily be associated with poor socio-economic status of the poor.

About 73% of our population lives in rural areas of the country, where the basic amenities and health care services are dismal. India has a dubious distinction of being self-sufficient in food production while having the largest number (75 million) of 'under five' malnourished children in the world.

Table 5.15: Safe Drinking Water and Adequate Excreta Disposal Facilities

	Urban	*Rural*	*Total*
Population with Safe drinking water available hoursor within reasonable access	92.6%	72.3%	77.9%
Population with adequate excreta disposal facilities available(Toilet/latrines)	80.7%	18.9%	36.0%

Source: National Family Health Survey, 2nd Oct, 2000.

Some achievements & failures noted in the rural areas are:

- Infectious diseases continue to be a major cause of disease and death.
- Many such infection diseases are preventable.
- Small pox has been eradicated.
- The incident of diseases of like Cholera and Malaria have shown decline.
- Vaccination programmes have provided some protection bringing down the prevalence of certain vaccine preventable diseases.
- Neglect the girl child, its poor health and poor nutritional status are prevalent.
- Adverse sex ratio, 933 females per 1000 males, is alarming
- Prevalence of under-weight children below the age of 3years is 224% in rural areas against 21% in urban areas is equally alarming.
- Only 33.3% of deliveries are attended by trained personnel in rural areas in comparison to 73.5% in urban areas.

It is more than evident that the health situation in rural areas continues to be far from satisfactory and it results in major drawback in development work. In the revised National Health Policy of the Government of India there is a lot of emphasis given to comprehensive rural health care services. The Govt. takes concerted measures to combat communicable and non-communicable diseases at the national level. These programmes also reinforce the delivery of primary health care throughout the country. TB is an infectious caused by a bacterium, which spread through air. It affects people in their most productive years of life and associated with poverty, over crowding and malnutrition. Natinal Tuberculosis Control programme has been under implementation since 1962 with the objective of detecting effectively treating them. Like Natinal TB Control Programme various programmes has been into implementation time to time, these are:

National TB Control Programme (1962)

National Programme for the Control of Blindness (1976)
National Leprosy Control Programme (1955)
National Malaria Eradication Programme (1953, 1979)
National Filaria Control Programme (1997)
National Iodine Deficiency Disorders Control Programme (1962)
Medical care for Remote and Marginalized Tribal and Nomadic Communities
National Mental Health Programme
Family Welfare Services

India has been the first country adopts a National Family Planning Programme. Family welfare is a centrally sponsored programme. Although the schemes are implemented through the State Governments, the cost is borne entirely by the centre .Reproductive and Child Health Programme (1994).
Maternal Health.
Child Health.

Table 5.16: Health Status at a Glance

Item	*Year*	*status*
The no. of PHCs functioning in rural India	2001-02	
-sub centers		137292
-PHCs		22807
-CHCs		3027
The no. of hospital beds	Jan 1988	
• For the whole India		585889
• Urban		492820
• Rural		93069
The no. of hospital beds	Jan 1988	
• Whole India		665639
• Population per hospital bed		
Population per hospital bed	1988	1451
Hospital beds per 10,000 population	1988	6.9

Life expectancy	2000	64.6
Crude birth rate	2001	27.5
Crude death rate	2001	8.4
IMR	2001	66
MMR	1998	407
Deliveries attended by trained personal		
• Total	1995-96	42.3%
• Urban		73.5%
• Rural		33.5%
Women of child bearing age using family planning services	1998-99	48.2%
Eligible infants upto 1 year who are fully immunized	1998-99	34.5%
	2001	49.0%
Prevalence of low weight birth rate	-	
Weight (<2500 gms at birth)		
• Total	1995-96	23%
• Urban		21%
• Rural		24%

Source: NFHS

A national review of the Immunization Programme in India (1989) covering 35 districts. It became a part of Reproductive and Child Health Programme (RCH) in 1997. By the end of March 2001, coverage levels had improved significantly.

Table 5.17: Immunization

Immunization status (% coverage)	*2000-01*
TT for pregnant mother	83.4
B.C.G.	102.7
Measles	92.1
D.PT	100.3
Polio	98.2

Source: Ministry of Health and Family Welfare.

Table 5.18: Decline in the Incidence of Diseases

Disease	*1987*	*2000*	*% decline*
Polio	28257	265	99.06
Diphtheria	12952	4352	66.4
Whopping cough	163786	26752	83.7
NNT	31844	2197	93.1
Measles	247519	25259	89.8

Source: Ministry of Health and Family Welfare (2001-2002).

There has been a marked improvement in certain segments of health status spelling the success of certain National Programmes like Pulse Polio Programme, RCH programme etc. There is an expensive infrastructure for providing primary health acre services at the grass root level and this is being continuously monitored,upgraded and reviewed by the Ministry of Health and Family Welfare.

The state of Tripura was a princely state and Maharaja Birbikram Kishore Manikya Bahadur was a last king. After the death of Maharaja Bikram Kishore Manikya Bahadur in May 1947, a council under the leadership of his widowed wife Maharani Kanchan Prabha devi took over the charge of the administration on behalf of minor Prince Kirit Bikram. The monarchy came to an end on 9th September, 1947 and Tripura was merged with the Indian Union as a part 'C'state, administered by the Chief Comissioner. Tripura became a Union Territory on 1st November 1956. The territorial council was formed on 15th August 1959, which was later dissolved and a Legislative Assembly with a council of ministers was formed in July, 1963. Tripura became a full fledged state in1972. Till 31st August 1970 the district administration was run by one Deputy Comissioner. On 1st September 1970, Tripura was divided into 3 districts, namely, North Tripura, South Tripura and West Tripura. Later the fourth district called Dhalai.Dhalai was created which started functioning from 16th April, 1995. Along with that there is one Tribal Autonomous District Council (TADC). At present there are 40 Rural Development Blocks and total 1062 villages both inside and outside TADC area.

According to provisional estimates of 2001 census, the

state's population stood at 31.91 lakh, with a population density of 304 persons per sq.km.(304 persons/KM2).The birth rate in the state is 16.5 per thousand which is lowest in North-east region and much lower than the national average of 25.8.Again its death rate is 5.4 per thousand which is much below than the all India level of 8.5.The significantly, the death rate of Tripura is second lowest after Mizoram. Of the states in the North-East, Tripura is the second most populated state after Assam, though in terms of area it is also the second smallest state. The scheduled tribes population of the state was reported to be 8.53 lakh in1991 that constituted 30.95 percent of the total population of the state. There has been a sharp decline in the ratio of tribal population during one century(53 percent in 1901 to 28 percent in1981).The population of the scheduled castes in the state has been reported to be 4.51 lakh which constitute 16.36 percent of the total population.

Total literacy rate of the state was 73.66 percent and specifically 81.47 percent male and 65.41 percent female were literate, according 2001 census. The economic infrastructure services such as power, energy, telecommunications, roads, railways, airlines, banking institutions etc. are the pre-conditions for development and growth of an economy. However, the infrastructure facility in the state of Tripura is not favorable both in terms of quality compared other parts of India. The Composite Infrastructure Index evolved by Centre for Monitoring Indian Economy (CMIE), based on availability of power, irrigation, roads, railways, post office, education, health and banking reveal an overall backwardness of the state in terms of infrastructural development. The assessment of CMIE for1991-92 rated Tripura as the most backward state in the entire nation, after Arunachal Pradesh. It is also to be noted that during 1989-90 to1991-92infrastructure index for Arunachal Pradesh improved from 31 to 43 where as the same index for Tripura, declined from 66 to 63, indicating a further worsening of the availability of infrastructure. Even though, the socio-economic infrastructure is poor in north-eastern states. However, Sikkim has been placed better in terms of socio-economic infrastructure index. Significantly, lowest index has been reported for the state of Tripura which demonstrates the poor socio-economic infrastructure status of the state.

Sadly, the level of public expenditure on Health and Family Health and Welfare in Tripura is low. In 2001-02,total expenditure on Health and Family Welfare was about 1.5 percent of GSDP. The share of the expenditure on rural health services and family welfare has remained nearly constant at 21 and 20 percent respectively. Despite an increase in per capita expenditure between 1993-94 and 2001-02,the share of expenditure on Health and Family Welfare has declined steadily from 2 percent in 1993-94 to 1.5 percent in 2001-02.This includes secondary and tertiary health are facilities, which also cater mainly to urban households but also to rural population around each urban centre.

The primary objective of SGSY remains the same, that of lifting the BPL families up to join APL group. Group based approach has been given priority over individual approach. Year wise physical performance of SHGy under SGSY is presented at below:

Table 5.19: Yearwise physical performance of SHGs under SGSY in terms of number of SHGs formed

Sl.No.	*Year*	*West*	*North*	*South*	*Dhalai*	*Total*
1.	1990-2000	267	17	118	16	418
2.	2000-2001	127	46	97	104	374
3.	2001-2002	351	170	174	144	839
4.	2002-2003	626	350	1154	261	2394
5.	2003-2004	4835	863	2372	634	8704

Profile of West Tripura District

Among the Four districts of Tripura, the West district of Tripura is densely populated. About two thirds of the population lives in the west district of Tripura. This district consisting of sixteen blocks with in its coverage area. The one and only municipal council of Tripura is in the west district District. The capital of Tripura is also in the West Tripura district. There are four nagar panchayat in this distrct. This district has taken initiative steps of the upliftment of the living status of the people of this district. All rural development blocks are tried their best for betterment.

Table 5.20

Block Name: BISHALGARH

Area (In sq. km)	329649
No. of Revenue Villages	Not Available
Population	180551
No. of Schools	131
No. of Govt. Hospitals	1
No. of Primary Health Centers	22
No. of Post Office	26
No. of Colleges	Not Available

Bishalgarh R.D Block jurisdiction was almost of the portion of Bishalgarh subdivision. Now the jurisdiction of Bishalgarh highway road and hilly region of west part. Another two blocks and Bishalgarh Sub-division are namely Bishalgarh R.D Block and Takarjala R.D Block. Apart from this, the Bishalgarh sub-division and block are also renounced for Kashbakalibari Temple at Madhupur Village Tourist spot of Sipahijala near Charilam. The placed PRI members and official staff of this block both are in constant touch with the rural people to alleviate poverty in large extent in block areas.

They have an ambition to gear up the socio-economic status of the rural people from the vicious circle of poverty.

At A Glance Self-Help Group Under Bishalgarh R.D. Block

1)	No. of formed during 04-05	:-	102 Nos.
2)	Total SHG up to date	:-	1081 Nos.
3)	Total BPL Group	:-	1042 Nos.
4)	Total APL group	:-	39 Nos.
	Total	:-	1081 Nos.
5)	Total Women member	:-	9225 Nos.
6)	Total Men member	:-	3695 Nos.
	Total	:-	12920 Nos.
7)	Total SC Member	:-	2924 Nos.
8)	Total ST Member	:-	2728 Nos.
9)	Total OBC Member	:-	1777 Nos.
10)	Minority Member	:-	3632 Nos.

11)	General Member	:-	1859 Nos.
12)	No. of Group 1st Gradation Passed	:-	384 Nos.
13)	No. of Group received revolving fund	:-	249 Nos.
14)	No. of Group yet to received revolving fund	:-	135 Nos.
15)	No. of Group passed 2nd Gradation	:-	77 Nos.
16)	No. of Group received Bank Loan	:-	(28+6) 34 Nos.
17)	No. of Group yet to received Bank Loan	:-	40 Nos.
18)	Total Corpus	:-	64.21 Lakhs
	a) Educational qualification	:-	List enclosed
	b) No. of Group involved Sericulture	:-	12 Nos.
	c) No. of Group involved in Pig Firm	:-	45 Nos.
	d) No. of Group involved in Fish Cultivation	:-	65 Nos.
	e) No. of Group involved in Poultry	:-	58 Nos.
	f) No. of Group involved in inegitable Cultivation	:-	88 Nos.
	g) No. of Group involved in Cane and Bamboo	:-	45 Nos.
	h) No. of Group involved in Other activities	:-	119 Nos.
	i) No. of Group involved in any activities	:-	620 Nos.
	j) No. of Group defunct	:-	29 Nos.
	Total	:-	1081 nos.

Health Indicators of Tripura

The Total Fertility Rate of the State in NA. The Infant Mortality Rate is 31 and Maternal Mortality Ratio is NA(SRS 2001-03). The Sex Ratio in the State is 948 (as compared to 933 for the country). Comparative figures of major health and demographic indicators are as follows:

Table 5.21: Demographic Socio-Economic and Health Profile of Tripura State as Compared to India Figures

S No.	*Item*	*Tripura*	*India*
1	Total population (Census 2001) (in million)	3.20	1028.61
2	Decadal Growth (Census 2001) (%)	16.03	21.54
3	Crude Birth Rate (SRS2005)	16.0	23.8
4	Crude Death Rate (SRS2005)	5.7	7.6
5	Total fertility Rate (SRS2004)	NA	2.9
6	Infant Mortality Rate (SRS2005)	31	58
7	Maternal Mortality Ratio (SRS2001-2003)	NA	301
8	Sex Ratio (Census 2001)	948	933
9	Population below Poverty line (%)	34.44	26.10
10	Scheduled caste population (in million)	0.56	166.64
11	Scheduled Tribe population (in million)	0.99	84.33
12	Female Literacy Rate (Census 2001) (%)	65.41	54.28

Table 5.22: Health Infrastructure of Tripura

Item	*Required*	*In Position*	*Shortfall*
Sub-centre	659	539	120
Primary Health Centre	104	73	31
Community Health Centre	26	10	16
Multipurpose Worker(Female)/ANM	612	593	19
Health Worker(Male)/MPW(m)	539	268	271
Health Assistants(Female)/LHV	73	62	11
Health Assistants(Male)	73	152	-
Doctor at PHCs	73	152	-
Surgeons	10	0	10
Obstetricians &Gynecologists	10	0	10
Physicians	10	2	8
Pediatricians	10	0	10
Total specialists at CHCs	40	2	38
Radiographers	10	4	6
Pharmacist	83	56	27
Laboratory Technicians	83	42	41
Nurse Midwife	143	268	-

Source: RHS Bulletin, March 2006, M/o Health & F.W., GOI.

Table 5.23: The other Health Institutions in the state are detailed as under:

Medical College	2
District Hospitals	2
Referral Hospitals	-
City Family Welfare Centre	-
Rural Dispensaries	-
Ayurvedic Hospitals	1
Ayurvedic Dispensaries	40
Unani Hospitals	-
Unani Dispensaries	-
Homeopathic Hospitals	9
Homeopathic Dispensary	66

Table 5.24: Caste-Age-Sex Composition of the Households

Sl. No.	Category	Caste of the Households					Age(in years)				SEX	
		ST	SC	OBC	GEN	RM	18-35	36-45	45-60	60& above	Male	Female
1.	SHG	-	11	32	12	-	26	14	7	6	2	53
2.	Non-SHG	-	17	20	15	3	31	5	2	17	-	55
	Total	-	28	52	27	3	52	19	9	23	2	108

Source: Field Survey, 2007.

Table 5.25: Educational Level & Marital Status of the Households

Sl. No.	Category	Educational Qualification									Marital Status			
		Illiterate	Literate	Primary	Middle	High	Madhyamik	H.S (+2)	Graduate	PG	Single	Married	Unmarried	Widow
1.	SHG	10	25	7	11	-	2	-	-	-	-	52	2	1
2.	Non-SHG	17	8	11	19	-	-	-	-	-	-	54	-	-
	Total	27	33	18	30	-	2	-	-	-	-	106	2	2

Source: Field Survey, 2007.

The aforesaid table indicates the caste, age-group and sex composition of the surveyed SHG and non-SHG households. Among the 110 households 28.45% are from SC community and 20% SHG families are SC, 58.18% SHG members are from OBC category. On the other hand, in case of non-SHG families 30.1% are from SC families and 30.36% families are from OBC category. The age group composition of SHG and non-SHG families are categorized into 4 sub groups. 47.27% sample households are aged between 18-35yrs and 47.27% SHG members are also from 18-35yrs age group.56.36% non-SHG families are from 18-35yrs age group category.

Though the survey is aimed to the women SHG members and non-SHG women but only 2 persons are male who are from SHG group and rest are women.

The aforesaid table shows the educational level of the SHG and Non-SHG households. Among the total 110 samples 27, are illiterate, 33 are literate only 2 females are Madhyamik passed.

It is observed that among the SHG and Non-SHG families number of illiterate women are less in SHG families and the 2 Madhyamik passed females are present in SHG families not in Non-SHG families among 110 samples 106 females are married 2 females are unmarried and 2 females are widow.

The above represents the occupational pattern of the SHG and Non-SHG members. The occupational pattern of the households divided into five(5)categories, these are agrilabor(AL),daily labor(DL), cultivator(C), business (B) and science (S). 45.45% SHG and Non-SHG members are daily labors and it is their primary occupation. 9.09% are also daily labor and took it as their secondary occupation.

So, maximum SHG and Non-SHG families are daily labors and took it as their primary occupation and a very less percentage i.e., 10.91% are private and Govt. Service holders. The income source of the maximum households are not desirable and very poor. On the other hand, only a few percentages have secondary occupation along with their primary occupation.

Table 5.26: Primary & Secondary Occupation of the SHG & Non-SHG Members

Sl. No.	*Category*	*Primary Occupation*					*Secondary Occupation*				
		AL	*DL*	*C*	*B*	*S*	*AL*	*DL*	*C*	*B*	*S*
1	SHG	6	32	5	9	3	3	7	4	-	-
2	Non-SHG	7	18	8	15	9	4	3	2	7	-
	Total	13	50	13	24	12	7	10	6	7	-
	Percentage	11.81	45.45	11.81	21.82	10.91	16.36	9.09	5.46	6.36	-

Source: Field Survey, 2007.

Table 5.27: Sex-wise Number of School Going Children of the Households

Sl. No.	*Category*	*No. of Children*		*No. School-Going Children*	
		Daughter	*Son*	*Daughter*	*Son*
1.	SHG	60	69	49	56
2.	Non-SHG	38	47	27	42
	Total	98	116	76	98

Source: Field Survey, 2007.

The above table shows the number of children of the households .Among the total number of male-female children only 76 female children are school going and 98 male children are school going.

It can be said that among the SHG families the number of total children is 129 among the 49 female & 56 male school going children. In case of the Non-SHG families total number of children is 85; among them 27 female are school going & 42 male are school going. Total 60 children are female in SHG families and 69 are male children. In Non-SHG families 38 are female and 47 are male children.

The tables shows that among the 5 SHGs 80% SHGs are engaged in income generating activities and only 20% group has not adopt any income generating activity. But main target of SHG formation is to encourage self-independent and income generating activities with the use of locally available resources. Among the 5 SHGs 40% SHGs are practice weekly meetings and another 40% are practicing fortnightly meeting that is two group meetings in a month. Only 20% SHGs are practicing monthly group meeting.

In these different group meetings they discuss about different issues related to their group and social issues like health & family issues which very common to them.

This above mentioned table reflects the motivator of the different SHGs and the performance of the SHG satisfied the SHG members are not. Among the SHGs panchayat & NGO or volunteer are the main motivator of the SHG formation.94.54% SHG members are satisfied by their group activity and 90.90% SHg members agree that SHG can alleviate poverty.

Table 5.28: Performance of the SHG in Economic & Social Sector

Sl. No.	Name of the SHG	Frequency of Group-Meeting					Group Involved in Social Activity		Income Generating Activity(Group)	
		Weekly	Monthly	Fort nightly	Daily	Half yearly	Yes	No	Have	Have not
1		-	-	1	-	-	-	1	1	-
2		-	-	1	-	-	-	1	1	-
3		1	-	-	-	-	-	1	1	-
4		1	-	-	-	-	-	1	1	-
5		-	1	-	-	-	-	1	-	1
	Total	2	1	2	-	-	-	5	4	1

Source: Field Survey, 2007.

Table 5.29: Motivator & Performance of the SHGs

Sl. No.	*Motivator of the SHG Formation*						*Satisfied by SHG Performance*		*SHG Can Alleviate Poverty*	
	NGO/ Volunteer	*Panchayat*	*Block/DRDA*	*Relative*	*Friends*	*Others*	*Yes*	*No*	*Yes*	*No*
1.	1	-	-	-	-	-	12	-	12	-
2.	-	1	-	-	-	-	11	-	11	-
3.	-	-	1	-	-	-	10	-	8	2
4.	1	-	-	-	-	-	9	3	9	3
5.	-	1	-	-	-	-	10	-	10	-
Total	2	2	1	-	-	-	52	3	50	5

Source: Field Survey, 2007

So, maximum SHG members are satisfied with their activity & maximum members agree that SHG can able to alleviate poverty. The table presents that the performance of the SHG members are satisfactory and may also able to increase the income of the poor families.

Table 5.29: Decision Making of the SHG & Non-SHG Members

Sl. No.	*Decision-making of the Women in different issues*	*Opinion in Different Issues*			
		SHG		*Non-SHG*	
		Yes	*No*	*Yes*	*No*
1	Education of Children is important	43	12	46	9
2	Marriage of children in early age	52	3	50	5
3	Family planning needed	47	8	44	11
4	Family Expenditure	51	4	49	6
	Total	193	27	189	31
	Percentage	87.72	12.28	85.90	14.09

Source: Field Survey, 2007.

The above table represents the decision making of the SHG & Non-SHG households in different issues of the family affairs.

Among the SHG members 87.72% of them took decision regarding their family issues but in case of Non-SHG members this rate is 85.9%. So, there is not much difference in between SHG and Non-SHG members, regarding decision making regarding different issues related to family issues. So in making of different family issues SHG members are more vocal than non-SHG members.

Table 5.30: Mobility of SHG & Non-SHGs in Different Issues

Sl. No.	*Different Issues Related Women Mobility*	*Opinion about the Issues*			
		SHG		*Non-SHG*	
		Yes	*No*	*Yes*	*No*
1.	Increase in knowledge/ Information acquired	38	17	41	14
2.	Freely Speaking/Discussion	39	16	32	23
3.	To help/assist others	52	3	48	7
4.	Saving habit	55	-	39	16

5.	To do something independently	44	11	18	37
6.	Leadership quality	25	30	7	48
7.	Importance in the family decision	51	4	49	6
8.	Mentality to help others	52	3	49	6
9.	To work altogether	43	12	12	43
10.	Health/Child health	55	-	54	1
	Total	454	96	349	201
	Percentage	82.54	17.46	63.45	36.55

Source: Field Survey, 2007.

The aforesaid table represents the mobility pattern in SHG and Non-SHG members by different issues which are directly and indirectly affected the women's mobility.

Among the SHG members 82.54% SHG members have mobility than other and in Non-SHG members 63.45% is the percentage.

So, the decision making & the mobility of the women differs between SHG and Non-SHG members. There may be enough chance that the mobility of SHG members is increased due joining SHG.

Table 5.31: Increase in income & problem facing in joining SHG of the SHG members

S.N.	*Increase in Family income*		*Any Problem facing in joining SHG*		*For betterment of Group Performance place suggestion*	
	Yes	*No*	*Yes*	*No*	*Yes*	*No*
1	12	-	2	10	5	7
2	9	2	-	12	9	2
3	10	-	1	9	6	4
4	9	3	-	12	7	5
5	10	-	-	10	4	6
Total:	50	5	3	52	31	24

Source: Field Survey, 2007.

The above mention table represents that either the income of SHG families increase or not. Is their any problem facing by the SHG members in joining SHG or lnot. 90.9% families agrees that their family income has increased after joining

SHG. 94.54% SHG members have not faced any problem in joining SHG.

So, the maximum members of the SHG are willingly joining SHG. On the other hand, maximum members are fulfilling the main objective of the SHG formation. Because, maximum, SHG members something their group activity.

Table 5.32: Performance of SHG members in the group meeting

S.N.	*Regular attendance in meeting*		*Placement of opinion in group meeting*		*Acceptance of the Opinion by other members*	
	Yes	*No*	*Yes*	*No*	*Yes*	*No*
1	10	2	5	7	4	1
2	10	1	9	2	7	2
3	8	2	6	4	6	-
4	11	1	7	5	6	1
5	7	3	4	6	4	-
Total:	46	9	31	24	26	5
%age	83.64	16.36	56.37	43.63	83.87	16.13

Source: Field Survey, 2007.

The above table reflects the performance of the SHG members in their group activity by the indicators like regular attendance in meeting, opinion placement in the group meeting and the opinion accepted by the other group members.

Among the SHG members 83.64% members attend regular meeting, 56.37% place their opinion in group meeting and 83.87% of their opinions are accepted by the group members.

So, the average attendance of the SHG members in meetings are remarkable. But the opinion placement in meetings are not satisfactory. Though the other group members accepted their opinions are much more.

The above mentioned table 5.33 reflects the knowledge of TB among the surveyed households. TB is Preventable disease.

Table 5.33: Age-wise Response of the SHG Members regarding TB

Sl. No.	*Different aspect of Tuberculosis (TB)*	*Age wise response of the SHG members(yrs)*									
		18-30yrs		*31-45yrs*		*45-60yrs*		*60 & above*		*Total*	
		Yes	*%*	*Yes*	*%*	*Yes*	*%*	*Yes*	*%*	*Yes*	*%*
1.	TB is Preventable Disease	18	78.26	25	80.64	1	100	-	-	44	80
2.	BCG can able to protect TB	20	86.96	23	74.19	1	100	-	-	44	80
3.	TB can curable & preventable	16	69.56	24	77.42	1	100	-	-	41	74.54
4.	HIV person easily effected by TB	7	30.43	11	35.48	-	-	-	-	18	32.72
5.	TB need uninterrupted treatment	8	34.78	17	54.83	-	-	-	-	25	45.45

Source: Field Survey, 2007.

Table 5.34: Age-wise response of the Non-SHG members

Sl. No.	*Different aspect of Tuberculosis (TB)*	*Age wise response of the Non-SHG members (yrs)*									
		18-30yrs		*31-45yrs*		*45-60yrs*		*60 & above*		*Total*	
		Yes	*%*	*Yes*	*%*	*Yes*	*%*	*Yes*	*%*	*Yes*	*%*
1.	TB is Preventable Disease	26	81.25	5	45.45	10	83.83	-	-	41	74.54
2.	BCG can able to protect TB	29	90.62	9	81.81	7	58.33	-	-	45	81.81
3.	TB can curable & preventable	26	81.25	5	45.45	10	83.33	-	-	41	74.54
4.	HIV person easily effected by TB	7	21.87	3	27.27	6	50	-	-	16	29.09
5.	TB need uninterrupted treatment	17	53.12	4	36.36	6	50	-	-	27	49.09

Source: Field Survey, 2007.

Table 5.35: Age-wise response of the SHG members

Sl. No.	Different informations about Malaria	Age-wise response of the SHG members (yrs)									
		18-30yrs		31-45yrs		45-60yrs		60 & above		Total	
		Yes	%	Yes	%	Yes	%	Yes	%	Yes	%
1.	Anti-Malarial tablets for pregnant	16	26.08	5	16.13	-	-	-	-	11	20
2.	Use of Mosquito net	21	91.30	31	100	1	100	-	-	53	96.36
3.	Malarial paitent need more liquid food	5	21.74	13	41.93	-	-	-	-	18	32.72

Source: Field Survey, 2007.

Table 5.37: Age-wise response of the Non-SHG members

Sl. No.	Different informations about Malaria	Age-wise response of the Non-SHG members (yrs)									
		18-30yrs		31-45yrs		45-60yrs		60 & above		Total	
		Yes	%	Yes	%	Yes	%	Yes	%	Yes	%
1.	Anti-Malaria tablets for pregnant	6	18.75	2	18.18	1	8.33	-	-	9	16.36
2.	Use of Mosquito net	32	100	11	100	12	100	-	-	55	100
3.	Malarial patient need more liquid food	10	31.25	2	18.18	5	41.66	-	-	17	30.90

Source: Field Survey, 2007.

Table 5.36: Category of the Households

Sl. No.	Different Informations about Malaria disease	Category of the Households					
		SHG H/Hs		Non-SHG H/Hs		Total H/Hs	
		Yes	%	Yes	%	Yes	%
1.	Anti-Malarial tablets for pregnant	11	20	9	16.36	20	18.18
2.	Use of Mosquito-net	53	96.36	55	100	108	98.18
3.	Malarial patient need more liquid food	18	32.72	17	30.90	35	31.82

Source: Field Survey, 2007.

Table 5.38: Category of the Households

Sl. No.	HIV and AIDS related informations	Category of the Households					
		SHG H/Hs		Non-SHG H/Hs		Total H/Hs	
		Know	%	Know	%	Know	%
1.	AIDS is incurable disease caused by virus	50	90.90	48	87.27	98	89.09
2.	Knowledge of AIDS infection process	38	69.09	42	76.36	80	72.72
3.	Use of disposable or sterilized syringe	33	60	39	70.90	72	65.45
4.	HIV can infect the baby during pregnancy from parents	26	47.27	31	56.36	57	51.82
5.	HIV infected person should practice safe sex	31	56.36	36	65.45	67	60.90
6.	HIV patient can easily effected by TB	18	32.72	16	29.09	34	30.90

Source: Field Survey, 2007.

Table 5.40: Different aspects of Tuberculosis

Sl. No.	Different aspects of Tuberculosis (TB)	Category of the Households					
		SHG H/Hs		Non-SHG H/Hs		Total H/Hs	
		Yes	%	Yes	%	Yes	%
1.	TB is Preventable Disease	44	80	41	74.54	85	77.27
2.	BCG can protect TB	44	80	45	81.81	89	80.90

Table 5.39: Age-wise response of the SHG members

Sl. No.	*HIV & AIDS related informations*	*Age-wise response of the SHG members (yrs)*									
		18-30yrs		*31-45yrs*		*45-60yrs*		*60 & above*		*Total*	
		Yes	*%*	*Yes*	*%*	*Yes*	*%*	*Yes*	*%*	*Yes*	*%*
1.	AIDS is incurable disease caused by virus	21	91.30	29	93.55	-	-	-	-	50	90.90
2.	Knowledge of AIDS infection process	11	47.82	27	87.09	-	-	-	-	38	69.09
3.	HIV can infect the baby during pregnancy from parents	7	30.43	19	61.29	-	-	-	-	26	47.27
4.	Use of disposable or sterilized syringe	9	39.13	23	74.19	1	100	-	-	33	60
5.	HIV infected person should practice safe sex	13	56.52	18	58.06	-	-	-	-	31	56.36
6.	HIV patient can easily effected by TB	7	32.43	11	35.84	-	-	-	-	18	32.72

Source: Field Survey, 2007.

Table 5.41 HIV & AIDS related Awareness

Sl. No.	HIV & AIDS related informations	Age-wise response of the Non-SHG members (yrs)									
		18-30yrs		31-45yrs		45-60yrs		60 & above		Total	
		Yes	%	Yes	%	Yes	%	Yes	%	Yes	%
1.	AIDS is incurable disease caused by virus	29	90.62	10	90.90	9	75	-	-	48	87.27
2.	Knowledge of AIDS infection process	25	78.12	9	81.81	8	66.66	-	-	42	76.36
3.	HIV can infect the baby during pregnancy from parents	21	65.62	7	63.63	4	33.33	-	-	31	56.36
4.	Use of disposable or sterilized syringe	23	71.87	8	72.72	8	66.66	-	-	39	70.90
5.	HIV infected person should practice safe sex	22	68.75	9	81.81	5	41.66	-	-	36	65.45
6.	HIV patient can easily effected by TB	7	21.87	3	27.27	6	50	-	-	18	29.09

Source: Field Survey, 2007.

3.	TB can be curable	41	74.54	41	74.54	82	74.54
4.	HIV persons can be easily effected by TB	18	32.72	16	29.09	34	30.90
5.	TB need uninterrupted treatment	25	45.45	27	49.09	52	47.27

Source: Field Survey, 2007.

The above table shows the awareness about HIV & AIDS among the Non-SHG households, who are not joining SHG yet. Among them 87.27% women from different age groups know that AIDS is incurable disease caused by virus. The women from 18-45 yrs age group know about AIDS near about 90%. But a very less percentage of women know the patient can easily by TB. Among them 50% women from 45-60 yrs know this fact & 21.87% of 18-30 yrs age group knows this fact.

So, on an average, the women from 18-30 yrs and 31-45 yrs age-group know the about AIDS and HIV very well. 78.12% & 81.81% women from 18—30 yrs and 31-45 yrs age group know about the process of HIV infection.

Most of the teenagers and adult age groups and are informed about HIV/AIDS. It is also known to those groups about the ill effect of HIV and how it comes to the human body.

The table below shows the knowledge of diarrhea among surveyed households. Among the 110 sample size 95 no know that diarrhea patient need plenty of liquid, only 80.90% women know that breast feeding should continued during diarrhea and ORS should given to the child during diarrhea.

But in SHG families 87.27% know the importance of ORS during diarrhea and in non-SHG families 74.54% women know the fact. 85.45% SHG women & 87.27% of non-SHG women are knows that diarrhea patient needed plenty of liquid.

The knowledge of breastfeeding should continued during diarrhea is possible known very less percentage,83.63% from the total SHG women & 78.18% non-SHG women from the total non-SHG families.

Table 5.42: Some information regarding diarrhea

Sl. No.	Some Information regarding diarrhea	Response of the H/Hs regarding diarrhea					
		SHG H/Hs		Non-SHG H/Hs		Total H/Hs	
		Yes	%	Yes	%	Yes	%
1.	Diarrhea patient needed plenty of liquid	47	85.45	48	87.27	95	86.36
2	Breast-feeding should continued during diarrhea	46	83.63	43	78.18	89	80.90
3.	During diarrhea ORS given to the child	48	87.27	41	74.54	89	80.90

Source: Field survey, 2007.

This above mentioned table reflects the knowledge of diarrhea of the SHG and non SHG members according to their age-group. Among the SHG members 28nos are know that diarrhea patient needed plenty of liquids and aged between 31-45 years age. From 23 no of SHG members aged between18-30 years 22 members know the importance of ORS.

On the other hand among the non-SHG members 29 no members from 32 total members aged 18-30 years know that diarrhea patient needed plenty of liquid and only 4 members from 45-60 years know the fact. The members from 45-60 years only 3 members know the fact that breast feeding should continued during diarrhea and the necessity of ORS for the diarrhea patient.

This table helps to understand the knowledge of diarrhea among the SHG and Non SHG according their educational level, 2 members from matric level know that diarrhea patient need plenty of liquid ,ORS saline and breast feeding etc from the SHG members .Maximum people from literate level know the preventive steps of diarrhea mentioned in the table and in the middle school standard every one know the initiatives during diarrhea.

In case of Non-SHG member's primary and middle school level educated members know about the initiative taken during diarrhea and in both SHG & non-SHG members who are illiterate do not know the fact properly or in very less percentage.

Table 5.43: Some information regarding diarrhea

Sl. No.	Some information regarding diarrhea	Age wise response of the house holds											
		SHG house holds (age in years)						Non-SHG house holds (age in years)					
		18-30	31-45	46-60	60&above	Total	%	18-30	31-45	46-60	60&above	Total	%
1	Diarrhea patient needed plenty of liquid	19	28	-	-	47	85.45	29	15	4	-	48	86.36
2	Breast feeding should continued during diarrhea	20	25	1	-	46	83.63	23	17	3	-	43	80.90
3	During diarrhea ORS given to the child	22	25	1	-	48	87.27	21	17	3	-	41	80.90

Source: Field survey, 2007

Table 5.44: Some information regarding diarrhea

Sl. No.	Some information regarding diarrhea	SHG households							Non-SHG house holds						
		Literate	Illit-erate	Prim-ary	Middle	Matric	Total	%	Literate	Illit-erate	Prim-ary	Middle	Matric	Total	%
1	Diarrhea patient needed plenty of liquid	20	7	7	11	2	47	85.45	8	10	11	19	-	48	86.36
2	Breast feeding should continue during diarrhea	20	6	7	11	2	46	83.63	8	5	11	19	-	43	80.90
3	During diarrhea ORS given to the child	20	8	7	11	2	48	87.27	8	3	11	19	-	41	80.90

Source: Field survey, 2007.

Table 5.45: Sanitation and Hygiene

Sl. No.	Information regarding sanitation and hygiene	Response of the households					
		SHG H/Hs		Non-SHG H/Hs		Total H/Hs	
		Aware	%	Aware	%	Aware	%
1	Use of sanitary latrine	7	12.72	8	14.54	15	13.63
2	Use of soap for cleanliness	53	96.36	55	100	108	58.18
3	Use of drainage system	-	-	2	3.63	2	1.81
4	Use of boil/filter water	13	23.63	17	30.9	30	27.27

This above table depicted a comparative picture between SHG H/Hs and Non SHG H/Hs regarding sanitation hygiene .In this table four indicators are used for the study like sanitary latrine, Use of soap for cleanliness, Use of drainage system and Use of boil/filter water .In this above drawn table awareness of Non SHG H/Hs is higher than SHG H/Hs in terms of sanitation and hygiene, which is clearly shown through the statistical figures in the table.

This above mentioned table an age wise comparison between SHG house holds and Non-SHG house holds in terms of sanitary latrine, Use of soap for cleanliness, Use of drainage system and Use of boil/filter water. This table is showing the higher level of awareness among the Non-SHG house holds about sanitation and hygiene.

Table 5.47: Information regarding Child Immunization

Sl. No.	Information regarding child immunization	Response regarding immunization					
		SHG H/Hs		Non-SHG H/Hs		Total H/Hs	
		Yes	%	Yes	%	Yes	%
1.	Regular immunization of child	12	21.81	13	23.63	25	22.72
2.	Complete immunization of children	20	36.36	18	32.72	38	38.54
3.	During sickness immunization	5	9.09	4	7.27	9	8.18

Source: Field Survey, 2007.

The aforesaid table shows the child immunization of the SHG and Non-SHG households. Total 38.54% households have complete immunization of their children. Among the

Table 5.46: Information about Sanitation and Hygiene

Sl. No.	Some information regarding diarrhea	Age wise response of the house holds											
		SHG house holds (age in years)						Non-SHG house holds (age in years)					
		18-30	31-45	46-60	60&above	Total	%	18-30	31-45	46-60	60&above	Total	%
1	Use of sanitary latrine	4	2	1	-	7	12.72	5	3	-	-	8	14.54
2	Use of soap for cleanliness	23	29	1	-	53	96.36	32	11	12	-	55	100
3	Use of drainage system	-	-	-	-	-	-	2	-	-	-	2	3.63
4	Use of boil/filter water	8	5	-	-	13	23.63	9	5	3	-	17	30.9

Source: field survey, 2007.

Table 5.48: Information regarding Child Immunization

Sl. No.	Some information regarding diarrhea	Age wise response of the house holds (in yrs.)											
		SHG house holds (age in years)						Non-SHG house holds (age in years)					
		18-30	31-45	46-60	60&above	Total	%	18-30	31-45	46-60	60&above	Total	%
1.	Regular immunization of child	7	5	-	-	12	21.81	8	3	2	-	13	23.63
2.	Complete immunization of children	9	11	1	-	20	36.36	12	5	1	-	18	32.72
3.	During sickness immunization	3	2	-	-	5	9.09	2	2	-	-	4	7.27

Source: Field Survey, 2007.

Table 5.49: Information regarding Child Immunization

Sl. No.	Information regarding child immunization	Education level wise response of the Households													
		SHG households							Non-SHG house holds						
		Literate	Illit-erate	Prim-ary	Middle	Matric	Total	%	Literate	Illit-erate	Prim-ary	Middle	Matric	Total	%
1.	Regular immunization of child	1	-	2	7	2	12	21.81	3	-	4	6	-	13	23.63
2.	Complete immunization of children	1	-	4	13	2	20	36.36	6	1	5	6	-	18	32.72
3.	During sickness immunization	-	-	1	2	2	5	9.09	1	-	1	2	-	4	7.27

Source: Field Survey, 2007.

SHG and Non-SHG families only 22.72% have regular immunization. It is shocking that only 8.18% have immunized their children during illness/sickness.

Immunization children are important because it protects children from various diseases. Though maximum households have 0-14yrs children but the immunization of those children is not regular or incomplete.

The above mentioned table presents the age wise response of the households regarding immunization. Among the 55 households of SHG members and 55 Non-SHG members 36.36% and 32.72% members of the both category respectively complete their children's immunization and these households aged between 18-45yrs.On the other hand maximum percentage of SHG & Non-SHG households know that immunization is not possible during sickness.

So, the older or eldest women are not aware about their children immunization both in SHG and Non-SHG members. But the SHG members know much than Non-SHG members because their rate is high. The general awareness of the households regarding immunization is lass's clear that younger women know much than the elder women about immunization.

The above table represents the knowledge of immunization among SHG and Non-SHG members according to their educational level. The women who are educated much i.e. whose educational level are higher their knowledge about immunization is much. In SHG members, persons of primary to matriculation have given response higher. On the other hand, in case of Non-SHG members the picture is just like SHG members.

So, it is clear that the educational level is a great factor for the children immunization. If the mother of the children is educated than their awareness will be much than that of uneducated.

Table 5.50: Information regarding Mother's Immunization

Sl. No.	*Information regarding mother's immunization*	*Response of the total Households*					
		SHG H/Hs		*Non-SHG H/Hs*		*Total H/Hs*	
		Yes	*%*	*Yes*	*%*	*Yes*	*%*
1.	Tetanus immunization during pregnancy	49	89.09	43	78.18	92	83.63
2.	Adolescents complete tetanus immunization or not	47	85.45	41	74.54	88	80
3.	Important tetanus immunization	32	58.18	33	60	65	59.09

Source: Field Survey, 2007.

The table reflects the response of the sample households regarding immunization of the pregnant women.83.63% households in total have done tetanus immunization. But only 59.09% know the importance of the tetanus immunization.

The response among SHG and Non-SHG members, the SHG members know better than Non-SHG members.

The above table reveals that the total immunization of the sample household is better during pregnancy. Among them SHG members are know much than Non-SHG members .It may be due to join group and increase of the unability of the members as they join group.

The age wise response of the sample households regarding immunization during pregnancy shows that the younger members both in SHG and Non-SHG members done their immunization of during pregnancy compared to the older one. The members in between 18-30yrs & 31-45yrs age group are much aware than 46-60yrs and 60 & above age group members both in SHG and Non-SHG category.

So, the table concludes that the immunization during pregnancy have done by the younger individuals much than the elder members. The younger generation is know or aware much than aged women.

The aforesaid table reflects the responses of the households regarding immunization of the mother and during pregnancy.

Table 5.51: Information Regarding Mother's Immunization

Sl. No.	Information regarding mother's immunization	Age wise response of the house holds (in yrs.)											
		SHG H/Hs						Non-SHG H/Hs					
		18-30	31-45	46-60	60&above	Total	%	18-30	31-45	46-60	60&above	Total	%
1.	Tetanus immunization during pregnancy	19	30	-	-	49	89.09	23	18	2	-	43	78.18
2.	Adolescents complete tetanus immunization or not	18	29	-	-	47	85.45	22	16	3	-	41	74.54
3.	Important tetanus immunization	11	21	-	-	32	58.18	17	15	1	-	33	60

Source: Field Survey, 2007.

Table 5.52: Information Regarding Mother's Immunization

Sl. No.	Information regarding mother's immunization	Response according to their educational level													
		SHG households							Non-SHG house holds						
		Literate	Illiterate	Primary	Middle	Matric	Total	%	Literate	Illiterate	Primary	Middle	Matric	Total	%
1.	Tetanus immunization during pregnancy	22	7	7	11	2	49	89.09	9	7	15	12	-	43	78.18
2.	Adolescents immunization complete tetanus or not	23	5	6	11	2	47	85.45	13	5	12	11	-	41	74.54
3.	Important tetanus immunization	12	-	7	11	2	32	58.18	8	3	11	11	-	33	60

Source: Field Survey, 2007.

Here in case of SHG members 49 members done tetanus immunization during their pregnancy, the educational level of the members are madhyamik, middle school, primary, literater and very less are illiterate. 47 households done their adolescents tetanus immunization.

The Non-SHG members 43 numbers done their immunization during pregnancy. 41 numbers done adolescents tetanus immunization of their family.

So, the above figure of the table shows that the educational level of the women affects the awareness of them. Because educated persons are more aware of children or mother.

Table 5.53: Information regarding Pregnancy

Sl. No.	*Information regarding pregnancy*	*Response of the total Households*					
		SHG H/Hs		*Non-SHG H/Hs*		*Total H/Hs*	
		Yes	*%*	*Yes*	*%*	*Yes*	*%*
1.	Regular checkup	18	32.72	21	38.18	39	35.45
2.	Birth attendant by TBA	31	56.36	35	63.63	66	60
3.	Knowledge of early signs pregnancy of the adults	45	81.81	43	78.18	88	80
4.	During complications of pregnancy attend hospitals or not	39	70.9	41	74.54	80	72.72

Source: Field Survey, 2007.

The above table presents the health awareness of the surveyed households during pregnancy. The pre-natal care of the SHG and Non-SHG members regarding regular check up of the pregnant women is done by 35.45% households; among 32.72% by SHG members and 38.18% by Non-SHG members. The birth-attendant by TBA of the households are 60%; among 56.36% by SHG members and 63.63% by Non-SHG members. On the other hand knowledge of early symptom pregnancy of the adults of the households is 80%. 72.72% households attend hospitals during complications of pregnancy.

So, it is clear that the knowledge of pregnancy of the surveyed households is better. Only the regular check up of the pregnant women is much lower.

Table 5.54: Information regarding Pregnancy

Sl. No.	Information regarding mother's immunization	Age wise response of the house holds (in yrs.) SHG H/Hs 18-30	31-45	46-60	60&above	Total	%	Non-SHG H/Hs 18-30	31-45	46-60	60&above	Total	%
1.	Regular checkup	11	7	-	-	18	32.72	14	5	2	-	21	38.18
2.	Birth attendant by TBA	22	9	-	-	31	56.36	23	12	-	-	35	63.63
3.	Knowledge of early signs pregnancy of the adults	19	25	1	-	45	81.81	21	10	12	-	43	78.18
4.	During complications of pregnancy attend hospitals or not	12	26	1	-	39	70.90	21	9	11	-	41	74.54

Source: Field Survey, 2007.

Table 5.55: Information regarding Pregnancy

Sl. No.	Information regarding Pregnancy	Response according to their educational level: SHG households Literate	Illiterate	Primary	Middle	Matric	Total	%	Non-SHG house holds Literate	Illiterate	Primary	Middle	Matric	Total	%
1.	Regular checkup	2	-	6	8	2	18	32.72	5	2	8	6	-	21	38.18
2.	Birth attendant by TBA	8	3	7	11	2	31	56.36	15	5	8	7	-	35	63.63
3.	Knowledge of early signs pregnancy of the adults	16	7	9	11	2	45	81.81	14	6	9	8	-	43	78.18
4.	During complications of pregnancy attend hospitals or not	13	5	8	11	2	39	70.9	14	6	8	7	-	41	74.54

Source: Field Survey, 2007.

This table shows the response of the surveyed households according to age group regarding the health care during pregnancy. Among the SHG members 81.81% adults are know the early signs of pregnancy.70.9% households attend hospitals during complications of pregnancy. But only 32.72% has attended regular check up during pregnancy. The respondents of the survey households, who have given their response, are under the 18-30 yrs and 31-45yrs age group.

In case, of Non-SHG households 78.18% adults know the early signs of pregnancy. But the responses of the SHG members are better than Non-SHG member.

So, the better awareness of SHG members about pregnancy shows that the groups know much than Non-SHG member. This may be reason of group meetings. Because in group meeting, not only they discuss about their group activities but also discuss about their other common social and family issues.

This aforesaid table shows the response regarding health awareness during pregnancy of the households. The 81.81% SHG members response that the adults of the family know about the early signs of pregnancy among the most are educated from middle, madhyamik and literate level, primary level. In case of Non-SHG this rate is 78.18%.

32.72% of the SHG members and 38.18% do not check up regularly during pregnancy.

So, like other information about health care, this knowledge also influenced by educational level. So, the much educated much know about the health care.

This table presents the some general awareness of the respondent regarding sanitation Hygiene. In this table the responses of the sample presents according to their educational qualification.

Among SHG households and Non-SHG households 96.36% & 100% families use soap for cleanliness. But among the two type of households 12.72% & 14.54% families of SHG and Non-SHG households have sanitary latrine.

But this table does not reflect any relation in educational level & sanitation & latrine. These factors are mainly affected by the economic status of the households.

Table: 5.56: Information about child Health

Sl. No.	*Information about child health*	*Response of the Households*					
		SHG H/Hs		*Non-SHG H/Hs*		*Total H/Hs*	
		Have knowledge	*%*	*Have knowledge*	*%*	*Have knowledge*	*%*
1.	Weight child after every 2-3 months	13	32.63	17	30.9	30	27.27
2.	Need of food 3 times a day for 3 yrs age of child	51	92.72	48	87.27	99	90
3.	Knowledge of Vit-A containing food	25	45.45	23	41.8	48	43.63
4.	During & after illness child need extra meal	49	89.09	47	85.45	96	87.27
5.	For development of child playing is important	43	78.18	41	74.54	84	76.36

Source: Field Survey, 2007.

The above mentioned table represents the information about child health of the SHG and Non-SHG households. 90% households give 3 times food to their 3yrs age of child. 87.27% surveyed households give extra meal during and after illness of their children. But only 27.27% households weight their child after every 2-3 months.

So, the surveyed households have some basic idea about the child health but they do not the some technical and modern concepts of child health or child rearing.

This aforesaid table shows the relationship in between child health and the experienced of the women.

Maximum aged person are traditionally rare their child, they very less information about modern and proper raring of children. But respondent in between 18-45yrs are know much in this regard.

This table is showing awareness level about child health between SHG H/S and Non-SHG H/S. In this table a comparison between Non-SHG members and SHG members according their educational level. The average response of the both group are same.

So, there basic difference in these two groups. But the educated women much aware then uneducated or less educated about their child health.

Table: 5.56: Information about Sanitation & Hygiene

Sl. No.	Information about Sanitation and Hygiene	Response of the H/Hs according to their educational level: SHG households: Literate	Illiterate	Primary	Middle	Matric	Total	%	Non-SHG house holds: Literate	Illiterate	Primary	Middle	Matric	Total	%
1.	Use of sanitary latrine	1	2	2	1	1	7	12.72	-	3	3	2	-	8	14.54
2.	Use of soap for cleanliness	20	8	7	11	2	53	96.36	8	17	11	19	-	55	100
3.	Use of proper drainage system	-	-	1	1	-	-	-	-	-	1	1	-	2	3.63
4.	Use of boil/filter water	-	-	5	6	2	13	23.63	2	-	4	11	-	17	30.9

Source: Field Survey, 2007.

Table 5.57: Information about Child Health

Sl. No.	Information about child health	Age wise response of the house holds (in yrs.): SHG H/Hs: 18-30	31-45	46-60	60& above	Total	%	Non-SHG H/Hs: 18-30	31-45	46-60	60 & above	Total	%
1.	Weight child after every 2-3 months	9	4	-	-	13		11	4	2	-	17	30.9
2.	Need of food 3 times a day for 3 yrs age of child	23	28	-	-	51	23.63	28	9	11	-	48	87.27
3.	Knowledge of Vit-A containing food	18	7	-	-	25	92.72	14	5	4	-	23	41.8
4.	During & after illness child need extra meal	20	29	-	-	49	45.45	26	9	12	-	47	85.45
5.	For development of child playing is important	16	27	-	-	43	789.098.18	21	9	11	-	41	74.54

Source: Field Survey, 2007.

Table 5.59: Some information regarding Pregnancy

Sl. No.	*Information regarding pregnancy*	*Response of the Households*					
		SHG H/Hs		*Non-SHG H/Hs*		*Total H/Hs*	
		Yes	*%*	*Yes*	*%*	*Yes*	*%*
1	Good health of female child in teen age & childhood is better for pregnancy	7	12.72	6	10.9	13	11.81
2	Smoking/taking alcohol/ drug is harmful for pregnant	8	14.54	9	16.36	17	15.45
3	Safe child bearing age is 18-35 yrs	4	7.27	2	3.63	6	5.45
4	More food & main 3 categorised food	5	9.09	4	7.27	9	8.18

Source: Field survey, 2007.

The aforesaid table presents some responses of the SHG & Non SHG members. The indicators used in this table are mainly some awareness during pregnancy. Like smoking, alcohol are injurious for pregnant, safe child bearing age is in between 18-35 yrs . Yellow green and white food are needed much for pregnant.

15.45 % surveyed household know that smoking, taking alcohol & drug are harmful for pregnancy. Only 5.45% are known that 18-35 years age group is safe child bearing age oof mother.

So the table reflects that the knowledge of pregnancy related issues are very less among the surveyed households.

The above table shows the comparison in between SHG & Non SHG members according to their age group 14.54 % SHG and 16.36% Non SHG members have the knowledge that alcohol drug are harmful for pregnancy .12.72% SHG and 10.9% non SHG members have the knowledge that good health of female child in teen age and child bearing age group is better for pregnancy period .The maximum response are collect from the 18-35 tears age group and the very less no. of members from 45-60 years age group know those facts.

So, the above table can not reflects the much difference in between SHG & non SHG members .But the knowledge of pre natal care among the both SHG & non SHG members are very less in percentage.

Table 5.58: Information about Child Health

Sl. No.	Information about Child Health	Response of the H/Hs according to their educational level													
		SHG households							Non-SHG house holds						
		Literate	Illiterate	Primary	Middle	Matric	Total	%	Literate	Illiterate	Primary	Middle	Matric	Total	%
1.	Weight child after every 2-3 months	2	-	5	4	2	13	23.63	3	1	4	9	-	17	30.9
2.	Need of food 3 times a day for 3 yrs age of child	18	5	-	9	2	51	92.72	7	11	11	19	-	48	87.27
3.	Knowledge of Vit-A containing food	6	1	7	9	2	25	45.45	2	2	6	13	-	23	41.8
4.	During & after illness child need extra meal	17	5	7	9	2	49	89.09	8	11	9	19	-	47	85.45
5.	For development of child playing is important	12	3	5	11	2	43	78.18	5	10	11	15	-	41	74.54

Source: Field Survey, 2007.

Table 5.60: Some Information Regarding Pregnancy

Sl. No.	Information about child health	Age wise response of the house holds (in yrs.)											
		SHG H/Hs						Non-SHG H/Hs					
		18-30	31-45	46-60	60& above	Total	%	18-30	31-45	46-60	60 & above	Total	%
1	Good health of female child in teen age & childhood is better for pregnancy	2	5	-	-	7	12.72	4	2	-	-	6	10.9
2	Smoking/taking alcohol/ drug is harmful for pregnant	4	4	-	-	8	14.54	6	3	-	-	9	16.36
3	Safe child bearing age is 18-35 yrs	3	1	-	-	4	7.27	2	-	-	-	2	3.63
4	More food & main 3 categorised food	3	2	-	-	5	9.09	4	-	-	-	4	7.27

Source: Field survey, 2007.

Table 5.60: Some Information Regarding Pregnancy

Sl. No.	Information regarding pregnancy	Response of the H/Hs according to their educational level													
		SHG households							Non-SHG house holds						
		Literate	Illit.	Prim.	Middle	Matric	Total	%	Literate	Illit.	Prim.	Middle	Matric	Total	%
1	Good health of female child in teen age & childhood is better for pregnancy	-	-	2	3	2	7	12.72	3	-	1	2	-	6	10.9
2	Smoking/taking alcohol/drug is harmful for pregnant	1	-	1	4	2	8	14.54	2	1	2	4	-	9	16.36
3	Safe child bearing age is 18-35 yrs	-	-	1	1	2	4	7.27	-	-	1	1	-	2	3.63
4	More food & main 3 categorised food	-	-	1	2	2	5	9.09	1	-	1	2	-	4	7.27

Source: Field survey, 2007.

The above mentioned table reflects the educational level of the respondent and also their responses regarding pregnancy .7.27% ,3.63%respectively SHG & non SHG members know that 18-35 years age is safe for child bearing.9.09 % &7.27% know that more food and main three category of foods are essential for pregnant women.

Table 5.61: Some information regarding Post Natal Care

Sl. No.	*Information regarding post-natal care*	*Opinion of the Households*					
		SHG H/Hs		*Non-SHG H/Hs*		*Total H/Hs*	
		Yes	*%*	*Yes*	*%*	*Yes*	*%*
1	Minimum 2 yrs spacing beetween 2 child	5	9.09	6	10.9	11	10
2	Breast milk feeding up to 6 month of age	52	94.54	53	96.36	105	95.45
3	Additional foods along with Breast milk after 6 month of age	54	68.18	55	100	109	99.09
4	Breast feeding avoids pregnancy up to 6 months	27	49.09	21	38.18	48	43.63

Source: Field survey, 2007.

The afore said table presents that the Knowledge of post natal care among the SHG and Non-SHG members. 99.09% from SHG and 98.18% non-SHG members know that additional foods along breast milk after 6 months age of child. 94.54% & 95.45 % are know that breast milk feeding up to minimum 6 months of age of child. Only 10% respondent are agree that minimum 2 years spacing between two child is essential. 43.63% only know that breast feeding can avoid pregnancy up to 6 months.

So it is clear that the both SHG and non SHG members have some good knowledge regarding post natal care of women.

Major Findings

The village is dominated by OBC followed by SC and general caste.

It is observed that among the SHG and Non-SHG families, number of illiterate women is less in SHG families.

Maximum SHG and Non-SHG families are daily labors and took it as their primary occupation and a very less percentage i.e., 10.91% are private and Govt. Service holders. The income source of the maximum households is not desirable and very poor. On the other hand, only a few percentages have secondary occupation along with their primary occupation.

Most SHGs are engaged in income generating activities and only 20% group has not adopted any income generating activity. But main target of SHG formation is to encourage self-independent and income generating activities with the use of locally available resources.

In different group meetings they discuss about different issues related to their group and social issues like health & family issues which very common to them.

Maximum SHG members are satisfied with their activity & maximum members agree that SHG can able to alleviate poverty.

There is not much difference in between SHG and Non-SHG members, regarding decision making regarding different issues related to family issues. In making of different family issues SHG members are more vocal than non-SHG members.

The decision making & the mobility of the women differs between SHG and Non-SHG members. There may be enough chance that the mobility of SHG members is increased due joining SHG.

Most of the families (90.9%) agree that their family income has increased after joining SHG, 94.54% SHG members have not faced any problem in joining SHG. So, the maximum members of the SHG are willingly joining SHG. On the other hand, maximum members are fulfilling the main objective of the SHG formation. Because, maximum, SHG members something their group activity.

The women from 18-30 yrs and 31-45 yrs age-group know the about AIDS and HIV very well. 78:12% & 81.81% women from 18-30 yrs and 31-45 yrs age group know about the process of HIV infection. Most of the teenagers and adult age groups and are informed about HIV/AIDS. It is also known to those groups about the ill effect of HIV and how it comes to the human body.

In SHG families 87.27% know the importance of ORS during diarrhea and in non-SHG families 74.54% women know the fact. 85.45% SHG women & 87.27% of non-SHG women are knows that diarrhea patient needed plenty of liquid.

The knowledge of breastfeeding should continued during diarrhea is possible known very less percentage, 83.63% from the total SHG women & 78.18% non-SHG women from the total non-SHG families.

On the other hand among the non-SHG members, 91% members aged 18-30 years know that diarrhea patient needed plenty of liquid and only 8% members from 45-60 years know the fact. The members from 45-60 years only 6% members know the fact that breast feeding should continued during diarrhea and the necessity of ORS for the diarrhea patient.

To examine the comparative picture between SHG H/Hs and Non SHG H/Hs regarding sanitation hygiene, four indicators are used for the study like sanitary latrine, Use of soap for cleanliness, Use of drainage system and Use of boil/filter water. It is observed that awareness of Non SHG H/Hs is higher than SHG H/Hs in terms of sanitation and hygiene.

Table 5.62: Child Immunisation in SHG and Non-SHG families

Sl. No.	*Information regarding Child immunization*	*Response of the Households* *SHG H/Hs Percentage (%)*	*Non-SHG H/Hs Percentage (%)*	*Total H/Hs Percentage (%)*
	Regular immunization of child	21.81	23.63	22.72
	Complete immunization of children	36.36	32.72	38.54
	During sickness immunization	9.09	7.27	8.18

Source: Field Survey, 2007.

The aforesaid table shows the child immunization of the SHG and Non-SHG households. Total 38.54% households have completed immunization of their children. Among the SHG and Non-SHG families only 22.72% have regular immunization. It is shocking that only 8.18% have immunized their children during illness/sickness.

Immunization children are important because it protects children from various diseases. Though maximum households have 0-14 yrs. children but the immunization of those children is not regular or incomplete.

The older or eldest women are not aware about their children immunization both in SHG and Non-SHG members. But the SHG members know much than Non-SHG members because their rate is high. The general awareness of the households regarding immunization is lass's clear that younger women know much than the elder women about immunization.

The women who are educated much i.e. whose educational level are higher their knowledge about immunization is much. In SHG members, persons of primary to matriculation have given response higher. On the other hand, in case of Non-SHG members the picture is just like SHG members. So, it is clear that the educational level is a great factor for the children immunization. If the mother of the children is educated than their awareness will be much than that of uneducated.

The response of the sample households regarding immunization of the pregnant women.83.63% households in total has done tetanus immunization. But only 59.09% know the importance of the tetanus immunization. The response among SHG and Non-SHG members, the SHG members know better than Non-SHG members.

The total immunization of the sample household is better during pregnancy. Among them SHG members are known much than Non-SHG members. It may be due to join group and increase of the inability of the members as they join group.

The immunization during pregnancy has done by the younger individuals much than the elder members. The younger generation is well known or aware much than aged women.

The educational level of the women affects the awareness of them. Because educated persons are more aware of children or mother.

The better awareness of SHG members about pregnancy shows that the groups know much than Non-SHG member. This may be reason of group meetings. Because in group meeting, they not only discuss about their group activities but also discuss about their other common social and family issues.

Regarding health awareness during pregnancy of the households, the 81.81% SHG members' response that the adults of the family know about the early signs of pregnancy among the most are educated from middle, madhyamik and literate level, primary level. In case of Non-SHG this rate is 78.18%, 32.72% of the SHG members and 38.18% do not check up regularly during pregnancy.

So, like other information about health care, this knowledge also influenced by educational level. So, the much educated much know about the health care.

Table 5.63: Information about Child Health

Sl. No.	*Information about child health*	*Response of the Households*		
		SHG H/Hs Have knowledge (%)	*Non-SHG H/Hs Have knowledge (%)*	*Total H/Hs Have knowledge (%)*
	Weight child after every 2-3	32.63	30.9	27.27
	Need of food 3 times a day for 3 yrs age of child	92.72	87.27	90
	Knowledge of Vit-A containing food	45.45	41.8	43.63
	During & after illness child need extra meal	89.09	85.45	87.27
	For development of child playing is important	78.18	74.54	76.36

Source: Field Survey, 2007.

The above mentioned table represents the information about child health of the SHG and Non- SHG households. 90% households give 3 times food to their 3 yrs age of child. 87.27% surveyed households give extra meal during and after illness of their children. But only 27.27% households weight their child after every 2-3 months.

So, the surveyed households have some basic idea about the child health but they do not the some technical and modern concepts of child health or child rearing.

Maximum aged person are traditionally rare their child, they very less information about modern and proper raring of children. But respondent in between 18-45 yrs are know much in this regard.

The aforesaid table presents some responses of the SHG & Non SHG members. The indicators used in this table are mainly some awareness during pregnancy. Like smoking, alcohol are injurious for pregnant, safe child bearing age is in between 18-35 yrs. Yellow green and white food are needed much for pregnant. 15.45 % surveyed household know that smoking, taking alcohol & drug are harmful for pregnancy. Only 5.45% are known that 18-35 years age group is safe child bearing age of mother. So the table reflects that the knowledge of pregnancy related issues are very less among the surveyed households.

The comparison in between SHG & Non SHG members according to their age group 14.54 % SHG and 16.36% Non SHG members have the knowledge that alcohol drug are harmful for pregnancy. 12.72% SHG and 10.9% non-SHG members have the knowledge that good health of female child in teen age and child bearing age group is better for pregnancy period. The maximum response are collect from the 18-35 tears age group and the very less no. of members from 45-60 years age group know those facts. So, it can not reflects the much difference in between SHG & non-SHG members. But the knowledge of pre natal care among the both SHG & non-SHG members are very less in percentage.

Table 5.64

Sl. No.	*Information regarding post natal care*	*Opinion of the Households*		
		SHG H/Hs %	*Non-SHG H/Hs* %	*Total H/Hs* %
	Minimum 2 yrs spacing between 2 child	9.09	10.9	10
	Breast milk feeding up to 6 month of age	94.54	96.36	95.45
	Additional foods along with Breast milk after 6 month of age	68.18	100	99.09
	Breast feeding avoids pregnancy up to 6 months	27 49.09	21 38.18	48 43.63

Source: Field survey, 2007.

The aforesaid table presents that the knowledge of post natal care among the SHG and Non SHG members. 99.09%

from SHG and 98.18% non SHG members know that additional foods along breast milk after 6 months age of child. 94.54% & 95.45 % are know that breast milk feeding up to minimum 6 months of age of child. Only 10% respondent are agree that minimum 2 years spacing between two child is essential. 43.63% only know that breast feeding can avoid pregnancy up to 6 months.

So it is clear that the both SHG and non SHG members have some good knowledge regarding post natal care of women.

Utilization of Human Resource plays a pivotal role in income generation of any country. Formation of SHGs is a viable alternative to achieve the objectives of rural development and to get community participation. SHGs are the welcome as well as effective tool to handle this problem of involving tradition bound, have attached women to contribute for the country's development.

PANCHAYAT AS AN INSTITUTION

The three-tier structure of panchayati raj institutions was brought into existence after the Mehta Committee Scheme was approved by the National Development Council (NDC) in January 1958. The NDC affirmed the objectives behind the introduction of democratic institutions at the district and block levels, and suggested that each state should work out the structure which suited its conditions best.

The new system of panchayati raj institutions was first adopted in Rajasthan and Andhra Pradesh in 1959, followed by Assam, Tamil Nadu and Karnataka in 1960, Maharashtra in 1962, and Gujarat and West Bengal in 1963 and 1964 respectively. The new system was implemented without any reservations whatsoever in Gujarat and Maharashtra, and with some reservations in Rajasthan, Andhra Pradesh, Tamil Nadu and Assam. In the rest of the states, the response varied from reluctant implementation to dilution, diarchy and ritualism in the system. With the operationalisation of the 73rd Constitution Amendment, a three-tier structure of Panchayati raj institutions has been adopted all over the country.

Panchayati Raj Institutions

It was Gandhiji who realized the importance of village Panchayats as important instruments of rural development, and of promoting and nurturing democracy at the grassroots. He asserted that unless Panchayats were invested with adequate powers, villagers cannot have real Swaraj Article 40 in Para in of the Constitution of India was introduced at hi insistence. The article states that: 'The State shall take steps to organize village Panchayats and endow them with such powers and authority as may be necessary to enable them to function as units of self-government:

In January 1957, the GoI appointed a committee under the chairmanship of Balwantray Mehta to study the working of the Community Development Programme, and suggest how best it could be maintained and implemented. The committee recommended a three-tier system of local government, christened `Panchayati Raj' by Jawaharlal Nehru. At the grassroots or village level were to be formed village Panchayats. at the middle or block level were to be Panchayat Samitis and !it the apex or district level Zillā Parishads were to be formed. The new bodies were to have wide powers and adequate finance. The committee offered two broad directional thrusts: *(a)* it argued that there should be administrative decentralization for effective implementation of development programmes, and *(b)* the decentralized administrative system should be under the control of elected bodies.

The three-tier structure of Panchayati raj institutions was brought into existence after the Mehta Committee scheme was approved by the National Development Council (NDC) in January 1958. The NDC affirmed the objectives behind the introduction of democratic institutions at the district and block levels, and suggested that each state should work out the structure which suited its conditions best.

The new system of Panchayati Raj Institutions (PRIs) was first adopted in Rajasthan and Andhra Pradesh in 1959, and thus PRIs have been in existence in India since then. However, there were inter-state variations in structural pattern, tenure and responsibilities entrusted to them. With a view to grant constitutional status to PRIs in the country and to bring about uniformity, the Indian Parliament passed the Constitution (73rd Amendment) Act, 1992 in December 1992. This act came into force with effect from 24 April 1993. It envisages the establishment of Panchayats as units of local self-government in all states and union territories, except the tribal areas in the states of Nagaland, Meghalaya and Mizoram, and certain other scheduled areas. Subsequently, in December 1996, the provisions of the 73rd Amendment were extended to the tribal and other scheduled areas also through an act of Parliament. Adequate powers and responsibilities would be devolved upon the PRIs at the appropriate levels, to enable them to prepare and implement schemes for economic development and social justice, as entrusted to them under the items listed in the Eleventh Schedule to the Constitution. Significantly, the 73rd Amendment does not have a provision for constitution of gram sabhas, but their powers and functions have to be specified by the state legislatures. However, in the extended act, constitution of gram sabhas is mandatory.

The salient features of the Constitution (73rd Amendment) Act, 1992 are as follows: *(a)* the Gram Sabha has been envisaged as the foundation of the Panchayati raj system. It shall perform such functions and exercise such powers as may be entrusted to it by the state legislatures. *(b)* There shall be three tiers of Panchayats, at the village, intermediate and district levels. Only states having population not exceeding 20 lakhs will have the discretion to not constitute Panchayats at the intermediate level. *(c)* Seats in a Panchayat at every level are to be filled by direct election from territorial constituencies demarcated for this purpose. In addition, there would be ex officio members also, as provided in the state legislation. *(d)* Seats shall be reserved at every level of Panchayat for Scheduled Castes and Scheduled Tribes in proportion to their population in a given Panchayat area, and for women to the extent of not less than one third of the total number of seats. Reservation for offices of chairpersons of Panchayats at every level shall also be made for SC/ST, in proportion to the total number of chairpersons of Panchayats at each level as the population of the SC and ST in the state bears to the total population of the state, and for women to the extent of not less than one-third of the total number of offices of chairpersons in the Panchayats at each level. *(e)* The term office of Panchayats shall be for five years, and elections must be completed before the expiry of its duration; if dissolved earlier, elections must be completed within six months from the date of dissolution. *(f)* A States Finance Commission shall be constituted in every state, to go into the principles governing the distribution and devolution of financial resources between the Panchayats and states. *(g)* The superintendence, direction and control of the preparation of electoral rolls and conduct of all elections to Panchayats shall be vested in a state election commission. *(h)* The Eleventh Schedule has been added to the Constitution, which denotes: 29 subjects/functions which could be entrusted to the PRIs. Ejections to the PRIs in most states have been held. About 25 lakh people are expected to be in position in the PRIs, out of which one, third would be women. The central government is assisting the states in orienting the elected representatives and officials towards their new responsibilities through training.

The three tier organization system of Panchayat Raj institutes is briefly discussed in the following paragraphs:

An important feature of the Act is empowerment of the GPs to make bye-laws with the previous sanction of the prescribed authority. Similarly, the ZPs and PSs have been authorized to make regulations with the previous permission of the Government. The State Government will make model regulations and byr-laws for the Panchayat bodies which they , by resolation, may adopt(227). Although the State Government has a say in terms of approving the bye-laws and regulations, the initiative to frame them is in the hands of the elected representatives.

Table 5.65: Panchayat Raj System in west Tripura

Sl. no.	*Panchayati Raj*	*Total numbers*
1	No. of Zilla Parishads	4
2	No. of elected members of Zilla Parishads	82
3	No. of Panchayat Samiti	23
4	No. of elected Members of Panchayats Samiti	299
5	No. of Gram (outside ADC)	513
6	No. of elected members of Gram Panchayat (outside ADC)	5352
7	No. of Grams (inside ADC)	526

Table 5.66: West Tripura District at a Glance in Year 2005

Sl no.	*West Tripura District*	*Numbers*
1	Total	15,32,982
2	Male	7,85,579
3	Female	7,47,403
4	Urban	4,10,067
5	Rural	11,22,915
6	Scheduled Tribe	3,87,081
7	Scheduled Caste	2,95,698

Administration

West Tripura District has four sub-divisions: Sadar, Bishalgarh, Sonamura and Khowai

West Tripura District has 16 Blocks: Mohanpur, Hezamara, Jirania, Mandwi, Bishalgarh, Dukli, Jampuijala, Melaghar, Boxanagar, Kathalia, Khowai, Padmabhil, Tulashikar, Kalyanpur, Teliamura and Mungiakam.

Table 5.67: Padmabil Block West Tripura District

Sl. no.	*Name of the block*	*Village*
1	Padmabil	Akhrabari
2	Padmabil	Bagabil
3	Padmabil	Dakshin Padmabil
4	Padmabil	Dakshin R.C. Ghat
5	Padmabil	Gaya Manibari
6	Padmabil	Kshirod nagar
7	Padmabil	Pashim Belcherra
8	Padmabil	Paglabari
9	Padmabil	Purba Belcherra
10	Padmabil	Ramdayal Nagar
11	Padmabil	Rasaraj Nagar
12	Padmabil	Ratanpur
13	Padmabil	Tuichachin Bari
14	Padmabil	Upendra Nagar
15	Padmabil	Uttar Padmabil

Table 5.68: Kshirod Nagar Gram Panchayat

Ward No. 1	*Male*	*Female*	*Total*
Iswar Chandra Para	173	174	347
Ward No.2	*Male*	*Female*	*Total*
I. Jamudar Para	150	137	287

Table 5.69: Electricity

Electricity	*Yes*	*No*	*Total*
APL	13	20	33
BPL	12	35	47

Source: Field Survey, 2007.

From the chart we show that the 52% APL family's getting electricity and 36.36% are not getting electricity facilities. The BPL (48%) is getting facilities from government, which is called *kutirjyoti* and 63.63% are not getting.

If we analysis house wise then the picture are different, total 31.25% getting facilities and 88.75% are not getting.

Major percentage of households is not electrified, although *kutirjyoti* is implemented for giving electricity to the BPL families.

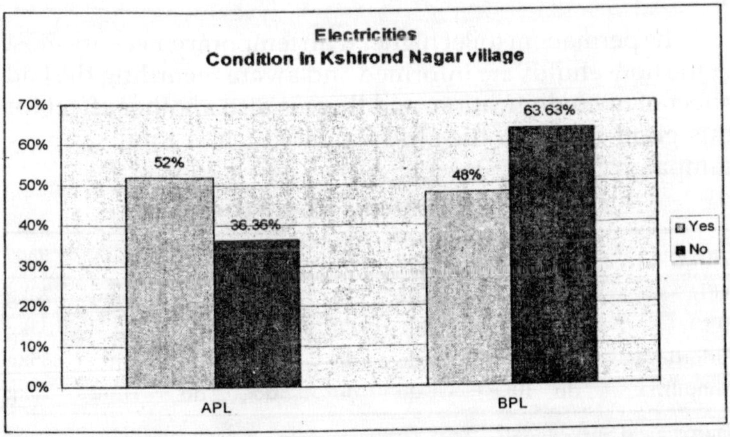

Table 5.70: Latrine

Type of toilet	*Number*	*Percentage*
Permanent	25	31.25
Temporary	55	68.75
Total	80	100

Source: Field Survey, 2007.

From the chart shows that out of 80 household 31.25% permanent, 68.75% temporary in this village.

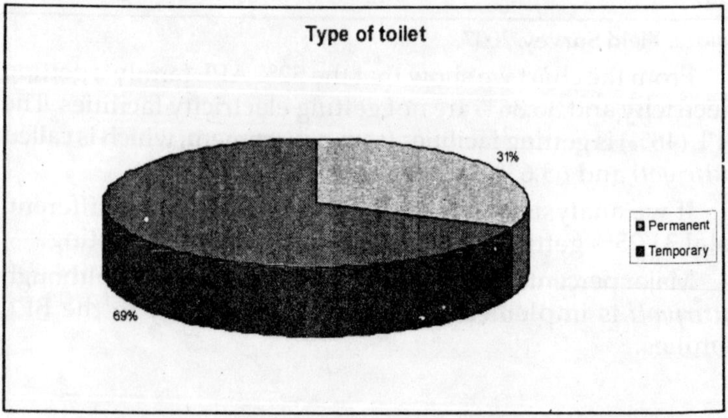

The permanent toilet higher than temporary, because most of the households are informed and aware regarding the bad effect of open deification, and there is also another effect for this good result in the study area which is total sanitary campaign (TSC).

Table 5.71: Items from ration

Category	*Rice*	*Rs.*	*Kerosin*	*Rs.*	*Sugar*	*Rs.*	*Monthly*	*Total*
APL	1kg	9.50	1litre	9.70	Per kg	13.50	2times	20kg
BPL	1kg	6.15	1litre	9.70	Per kg	do	do	35kg
Antordaya	1kg	3	do	do	do	do	1times	35kg
Annpurna	do	10kg	do	do	do	do	1times	10kg

Source: Field Survey, 2007.

The table shows that the items from ration there are getting different types like rice, kerosene, sugar, salt etc. but the APL families are getting in two times in a month total per kg 20, the price of APL families 1liter kerosene rate 9.70. The BPL families are getting two times total 35 kg per month. The price of rice's is 6.15 per kg and the price of kerosene per liter 4.25. The Antordaya are getting rice total 35kg per month and the price of rice 3. The prices of kerosene are same with the APL and BPL families. The Annapurna is getting rice total 10kg per month free of cost.

Livestock

Table 5.72: APL families' livestock

Category	*Number*	*Percentage*	*Total household*
Cattle	13	28.26	46
Goats	17	36.95	
Poultry(hen)	20	43.47	
Duck	6	13.04	
Pig	16	34.78	

Source: Field Survey, 2007.

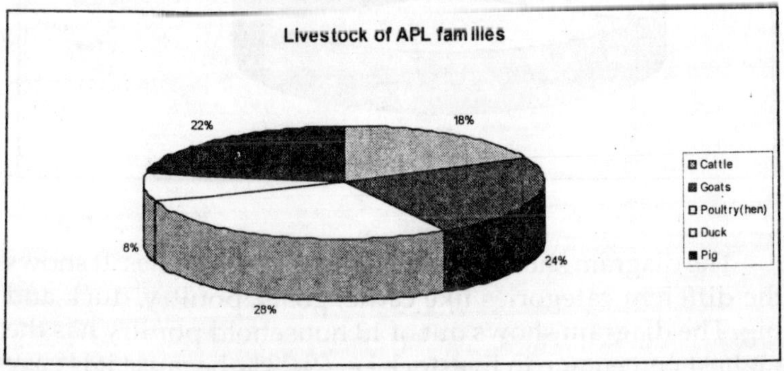

The diagram shows the livestock of APL family in different categories like cattle, goats, poultry (hen), duck, and pig. From this chart we can observe that out of 46 households poultry has the highest number i.e. 43.47% because it does not require much care. And out of 46 households there are only 13.04% of duck and it has the least percentage among those category.

In this area due to the scarcity of water the villagers were unable to rear it .And the rest category like goats have 36.95%, cattle 28.26%, and pig 34.78%.

Table 5.73: BPL families' Livestock

Category	*Number*	*Percentage*	*Total household*
Cattle	3	23.07	13
Goats	6	46.15	
Poultry(hen)	9	69.23	
Duck	2	15.38	
Pig	7	53.84	

Source: Field Survey, 2007.

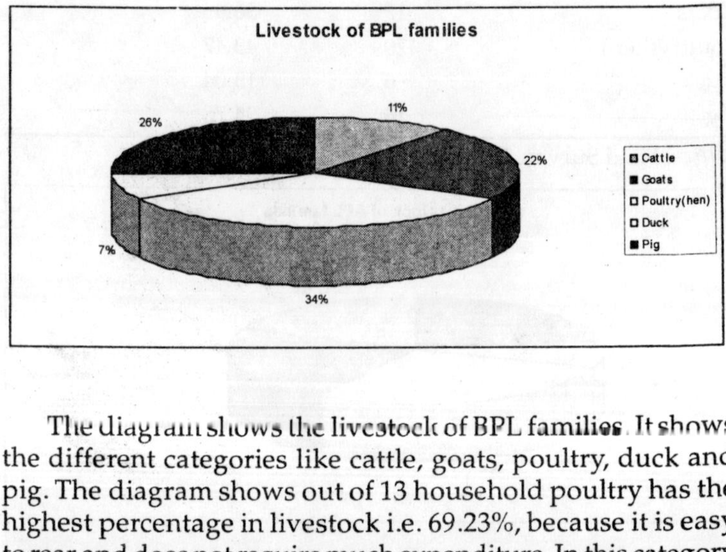

The diagram shows the livestock of BPL families. It shows the different categories like cattle, goats, poultry, duck and pig. The diagram shows out of 13 household poultry has the highest percentage in livestock i.e. 69.23%, because it is easy to rear and does not require much expenditure. In this category duck has the lowest percentage of rearing capacity i.e. only 15.38% out of 13 households. And the other category such as goats 46.155, cattle 23.07, and pig has 53.84%. As the BPL families can not afford they have limited number of livestock's.

Table 5.74: Annapuran families Livestock

Category	*Number*	*Percentage household*	*Total*
Cattle	Nil	0	9
Goats	3	33.33	
Poultry(hen)	5	55.55	
Duck	Nil	0	
Pig	4	44.44	

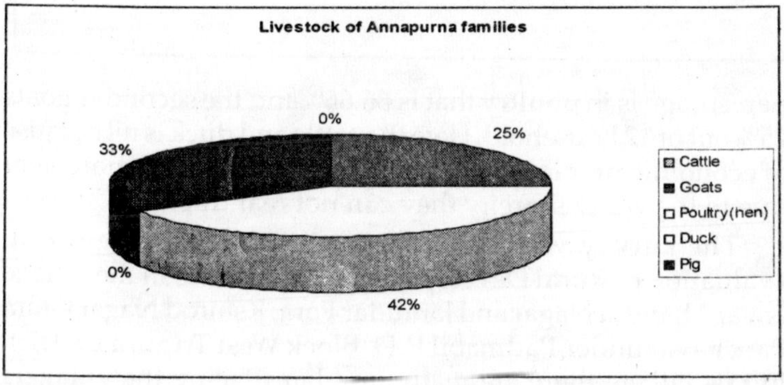

The diagram shows the livestock of Annapurna families in different category. In this diagram the highest number of percentage is in poultry that is 55.55% and the second is pig 44.44% out of 9 household. Here the cattle and duck is nil because of economic problem they were unable to buy and more over due to the water scarcity they can not rear duck.

Table 5.75: Antordaya families live stock

Category	*Number*	*Percentage household*	*Total*
Cattle	Nil	0	12
Goats	3	25	
Poultry(hen)	8	66.66	
Duck	Nil	0	
Pig	2	16.66	

The diagram shows the livestock of Antordaya families in different category. In this diagram the highest number of

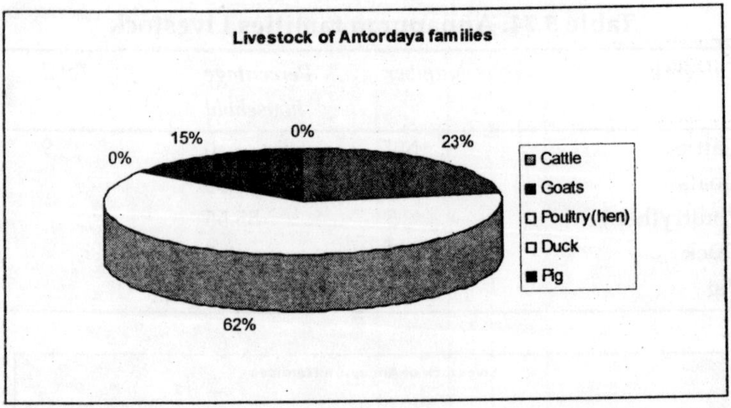

percentage is in poultry that is 66.66%and the second is goats 25% out of 12 household. Here the cattle and duck is nil because of economic problem they were unable to buy and more over due to the water scarcity they can not rear duck.

The survey was conducted with the purpose for an evaluation of Rural Development Programmes in the village Iswar Chandra Nagar and Jamudar Para, Kshirod Nagar Gram Panchayat under Padmabil R.D. Block West Tripura District. In this village there are many problems facing the villagers like water, irrigation, electrification, transport communication, and others.

Table 5.76: Family size

Category	*Male*	*Female*
Adult	196	178
Child	39	27

Source: Field Survey, 2007.

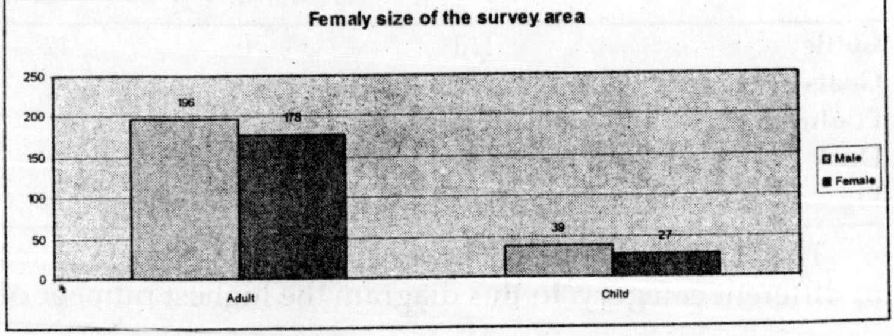

According to this chart we see that the adult male is more than adult female and also male child is more than female child.

Table 5.77: Education status of the Sample Households

Standard	*Male*	*Percentage (%)*	*Female*	*Percentage (%)*
Illiterate	26	16.35%	29	22.30%
I-V	27	16.98%	23	17.69%
V-X	67	42.13%	55	42.30%
X-XII	20	12.57%	11	8.46%
XII-B.A.	15	9.43%	8	6.15%
Graduate	4	2.51%	4	3.07%
Total	159	100	130	100

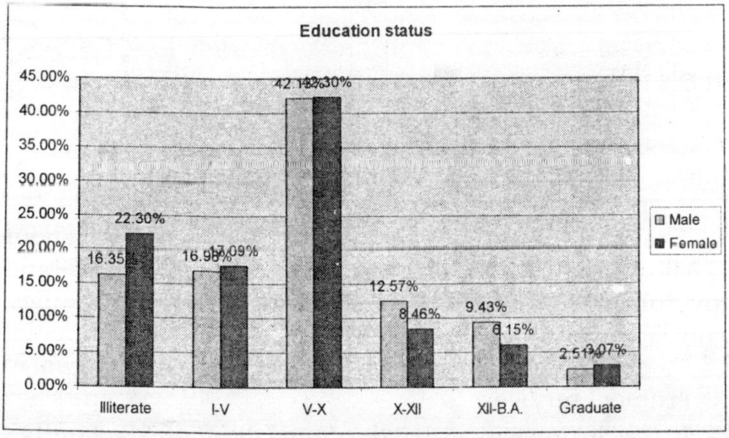

The chart shows that educational condition of the field area which is poor, so the family members cannot support to their child in education background. For this reason, they cannot go for higher education even the people of the study area have less literacy rate.

In conclusion it is found that the more students are under the group of class V-X.

Table 5.78: Occupation

Category	*APL*	*Percentage (%)*	*BPL*	*Percentage (%)*
Daily labour	15	32.60%	23	67.69%
Farmer	13	28.26%	7	20.58%
Business	4	8.69%	2	5.88%
Carpenter	2	4.34%	2	5.88%
Government Service	12	26.08%	Nil	0%
Total	46	100	34	100

Source: Field Survey, 2007.

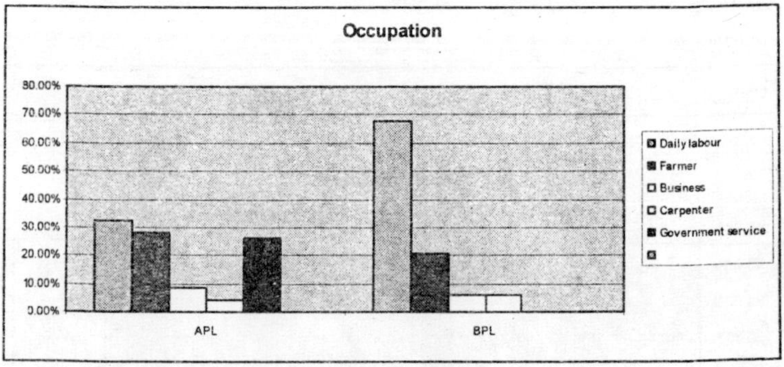

The chart shows that under the APL families, daily labour 32.60%, farmer 28.26%, business 8.69%, carpenter 4.34% and government service 26.08%. Where under the BPL families, daily labour 67.69%, farmer 20.58%, business 5.88%, carpenter 5.88% but there is no service person who is engaged in government service.

In conclusion we see that the daily labour of APL families higher than BPL families. The government service of APL families is very high and BPL families have no persons.

The chart shows that monthly income of APL families under the category of 500-1000, only 55% belong to this group, under 1000-1500 only 15% households belong and under the category of 1500-2000, only 4% belong and above 2000 out of 46 households 26%. The BPL families' monthly income, 76.92% are under the 500-1000 group, 23.07% house holds under 1000-1500. The Annapurna families' income is like; 88.88% under 500-1000 and 11.11% under 1000-1500. The Antordaya families'

Table 5.79: Monthly income

Monthly income Up to	*APL*	%	*BPL*	%	*Anna-purna*	%	*Antordaya*	%
500-1000	25	54.34%	10	76.92%	8	88.88%	11	91.66%
1000-1500	7	15.21%	3	23.07%	1	11.11%	1	8.33%
1500-2000	2	4.34%	Nil	Nil	Nil		Nil	
Above 2000	12	26.08%	Nil	Nil	Nil		nil	100%
Total	46	100%	13	100%	9	100%	12	

Source: Field Survey, 2007.

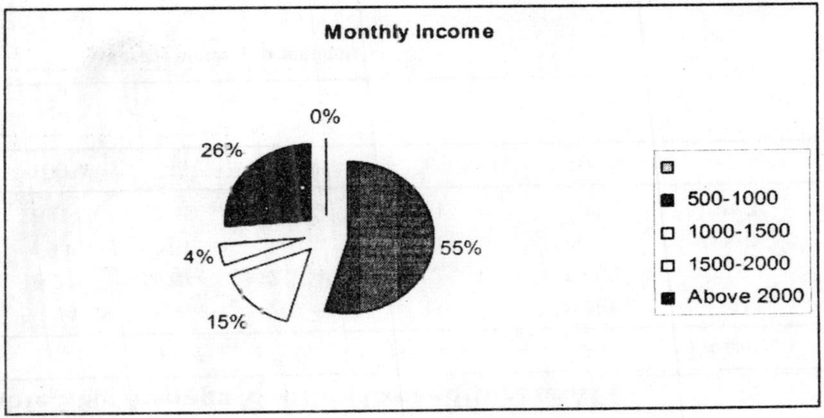

Table 5.80: Average Monthly Expenditure of APL

Monthly expenditure	*Food*	%	*Fuel*	%	*Transport*	%	*Education*	%
100-600	25	54.34%	36	78.26%	35	94.60%	31	86.11%
600-1100	7	15.21%	10	21.74%	2	5.40%	5	13.89%
1100-1600	2	4.34%	Nil	0%	Nil	0%	Nil	0%
Above -1600	12	26.08%	Nil	0%	Nil	0%	Nil	0%
Total	46	100%	46	100%	37	100%	36	100%

Source: Field Survey, 2007.

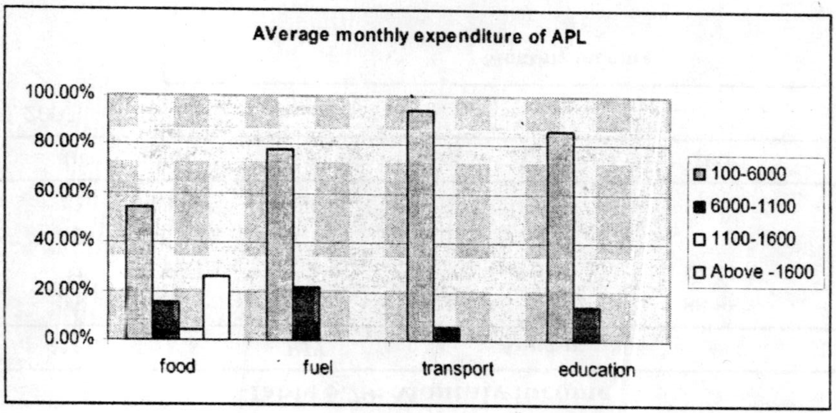

income is, 91.66% households under the income group of 500-1000 and 8.33% under the income group of 1000-1500.

In conclusion we can see that the family income of Antordaya is higher than Annapurna, income of Antordaya family is less than BPL, and obviously APL families' income is much higher than the BPL families.

The chart shows that the monthly expenditure of APL families in different activities like food, fuel, transport, and education. The monthly expenditure has been taken from 100 and above 1600. The monthly expenditure of food out of 46 households, 25 households expenditure is between 100- 600 and it is the highest expenditure. And the lowest expenditure is "between" 1100-1600. The monthly expenditure in fuel out of 46 there are 36 households expending between 100-600 and the lowest expenditure is 10 and the expenditure between above 1600 is nil due to the low income level. As in transport the 35 households which is the highest expenditure is "between"100-600 comprising 2 households. The villager does not require going for market to any where because mostly they grow some vegetables for their own. The monthly expenditure in education is 31 which are the highest out of 46 households. That is above 1600.

The chart shows that the average monthly expenditure of BPL shows different activities. The average monthly expenditure of food is high in "between" 600-1100, out of 13 household. The expenditure of fuel is 9. The expenditure of transport lies "between" 100-600 there are only 6 households and 600-1100 there are only 2 households expenditure in education. The educational status is poor and they do require but poor condition. The expenditure of transport also less, it lies "between" 100-600 only 8 households. The table shows the less amount of expenditure in every activity. Due to the backwards and poor condition the villagers were unable to come up.

Table 5.81: Average Monthly Expenditure of BPL

Monthly expenditure	*Food*	%	*Fuel*	%	*Transport*	%	*Education*	%
100-600	3	23.07%	9	100%	6	75%	10	76.93%
600-1100	8	61.53%	Nil	0%	2	25%	3	23.07%
1100-1600	1	7.70%	Nil	0%	Nil	0%	Nil	0%
Above -1600	1	7.70%	Nil	0%	Nil	0%	Nil	0%
Total	13	100%	9	100%	8	100%	13	100%

Source: Field Survey, 20C7.

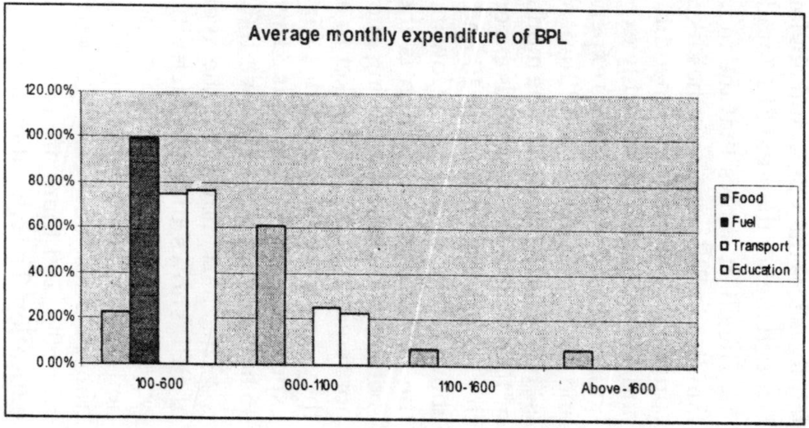

Table 5.82: Average Monthly Expenditure of Antordaya families

Monthly expenditure	*Food*	%	*Fuel*	%	*Transport*	%	*Education*	%
100-600	3	25%	12	100%	8	100%	11	91.67%
600-1100	7	58.33%	Nil	0%	Nil	0%	1	8.33%
1100-1600	2	16.67%	Nil	0%	Nil	0%	Nil	0%
Above -1600	Nil	0%	Nil	0%	Nil	0%	Nil	0%
Total	12	100%	12	100%	8	100%	12	100%

Source: Field Survey, 2C07.

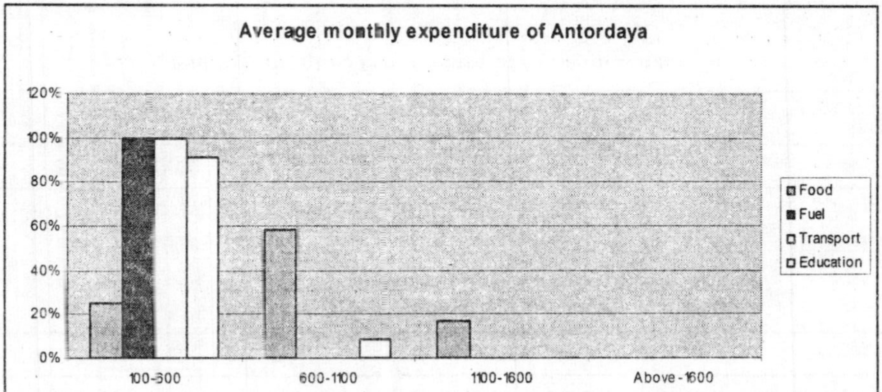

Table 5.83: Average Monthly Expenditure of Annapurana families

Monthly expenditure	*Food*	*%*	*Fuel*	*%*	*Transport*	*%*	*Education*	*%*
100-600	3	33.33%	9	100%	8	100%	8	100%
600-1100	5	55.55%	Nil	0%	Nil	0%	Nil	0%
1100-1600	1	11.11%	Nil	0%	Nil	0%	Nil	0%
Above -1600	Nil	0%	Nil	0%	Nil	0%	Nil	0%
Total	9	100%	9	100%	8	100%	8	100%

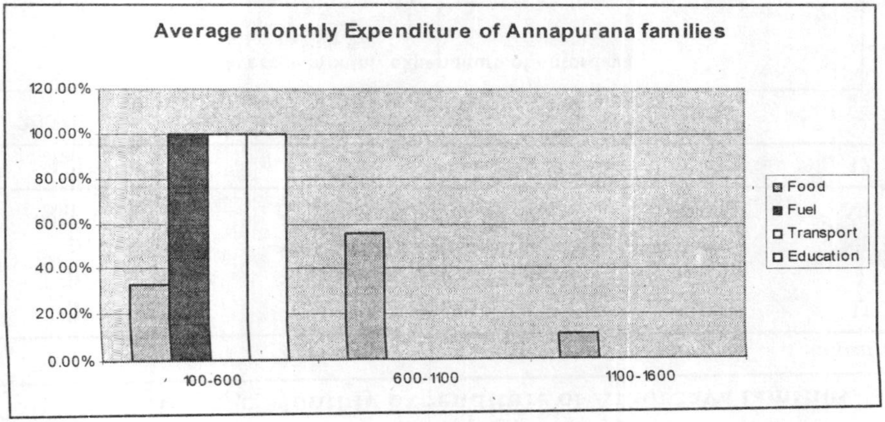

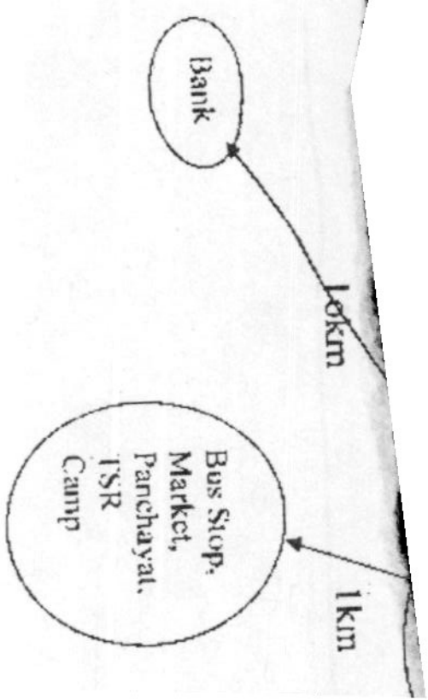

The chart shows that the average monthly expenditure of Antordaya shows different activities. The average monthly expenditure of food is high in "between" 600-1100, out of 12 household. The expenditure of fuel is 12. The expenditure of education lies "between" 100-600 there are only 12 households. The educational status is poor and they do not require much amount of expenditure. The expenditure of transport also less, it lies "between" 100-600 only 8 households. The table shows the less amount of expenditure in every activity. Due to the backwards and poor condition the villagers were unable to come up.

The chart shows the average monthly expenditure of Annapuran has been taken from 100-600 in their different activities. The number of households is 3 in food expending "between" 100-600, in fuel the number of households is 9 " between" 100-600, in education the number of household is 8 expending "between" 100-600, in transport 8 households. We can see that the condition of Annapurna having the lowest expenditure.

Exhibit;-1 **INSTITUTIONAL ANALYSIS**

Amenities from Iswar Chandra Nagar (distance in kms)

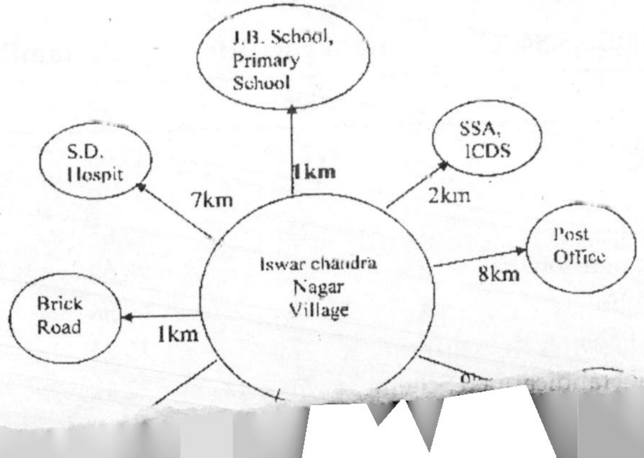

Exhibit: - 2
Amenities from Jamudar Para (distance in kms)

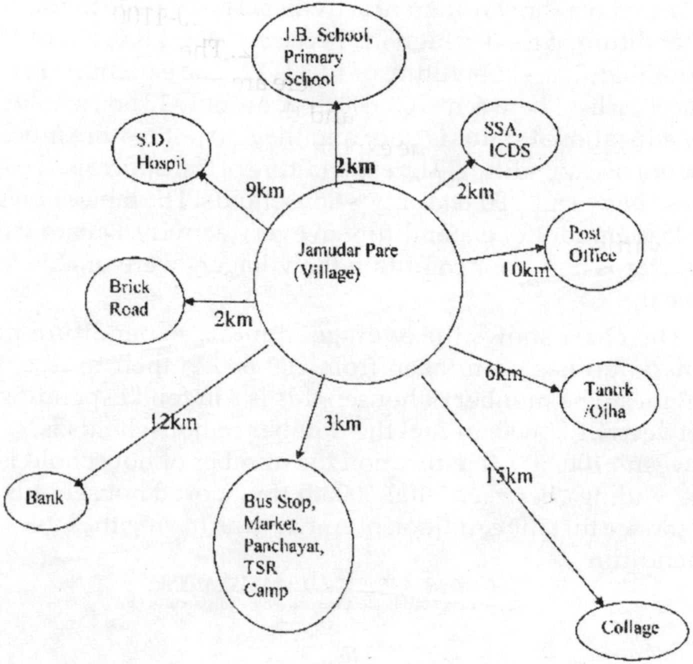

Table 5.84: Government Facilities of APL family

Facilities	*Number*	*Percentage*	*Total*
NREGA	21	45.65	46
IAY	Nil	0	
Midday meal	21	45.65	
Old age pension	12	26.08	
Pulse Polio	28	60.86	
Widow Pension	7	15.21	
Physical Handicappe Scheme	1	2.17	
		0	

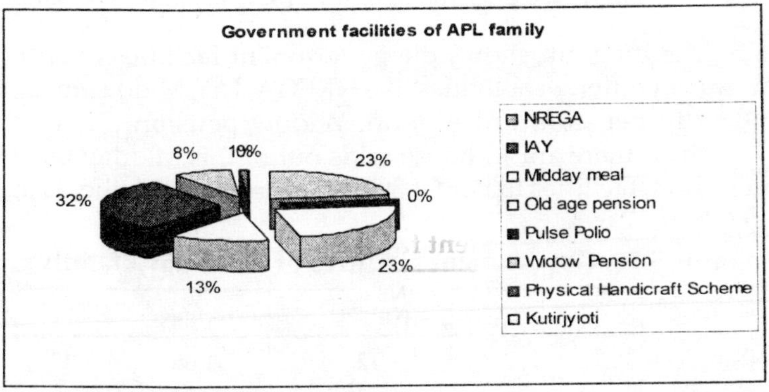

The diagram shows the government facilities of APL family in different activities like NREGA, IAY, Midday meal, Old age pension, Pulse polio, Widow pension, PH and Kutirjyoti . There are 46 households out of this Pulse polio gets more facilities that is 60.86% and the lowest facility is in PH that is 2.17%.

Table 5.85: Government facilities of BPL family

Facilities	*Number*	*Percentage*	*Total*
NREGA	11	84.61	13
IAY	2	15.38	
Midday meal	12	92.30	
Old age pension	2	15.38	
Pulse Polio	10	76.92	
Physical Handicraft Scheme	1	7.69	
Kutirjyoti	3	23.07	

Source: Field Survey, 2007.

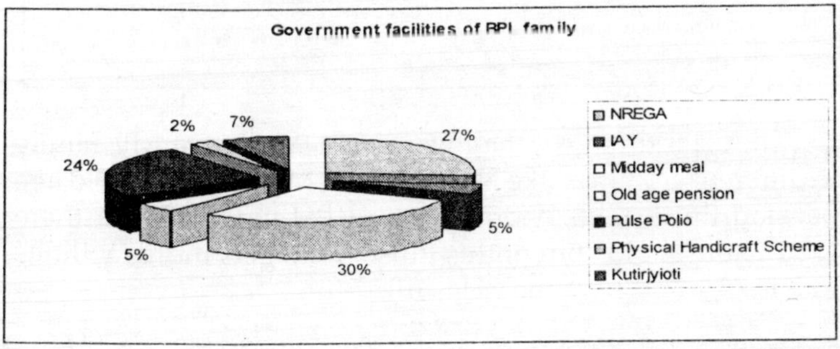

The diagram shows the government facilities of APL family in different activities like NREGA, IAY, Midday meal, Old age pension, Pulse polio, Widow pension, PH and Kutirjyoti there are 13 households out of this Midday meal gets more facilities that is 92.30% and the lowest facility is in PH that is 7.69%.

Table 5.86: Government facilities of Antordaya family

Facilities	*Number*	*Percentage*	*Total*
NREGA	12	41.66	12
IAY	3	25	
Midday meal	8	66.66	
Old age pension	4	33.33	
Pulse Polio	9	75	
Physical Handicraft Scheme	Nil	0	
Kutirjyoti	2	16.66	

Source: Field Survey, 2007.

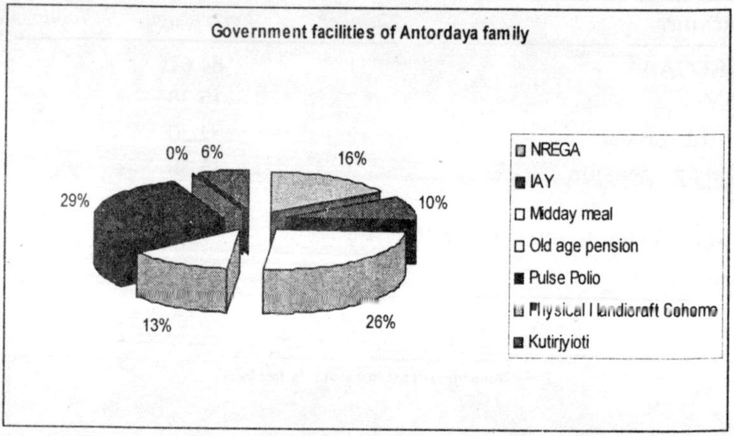

The diagram shows the government facilities of APL family in different activities like NREGA, IAY, Midday meal, Old age pension, Pulse polio, Widow pension, PH and Kutirjyoti .there are 12 households out of this Pulse polio gets more facilities that is 75% and here the PH is nil.

Table 5.87: Government facilities of Annapurna family

Category	*Number*	*Percentage*	*Total*
NREGA	9	100	9
IAY	1	11.11	
Midday meal	9	100	
Old age pension	3	33.33	
Pulse Polio	7	77.77	
Widow Pension	Nil	0	
Physical Handicraft Scheme	Nil	0	
Kutirjyioti	3	33.33	

Source: Field Survey, 2007.

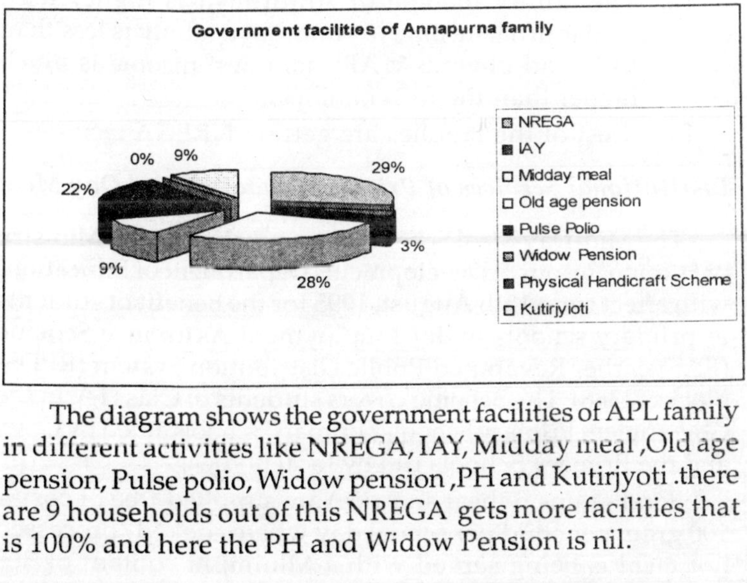

The diagram shows the government facilities of APL family in different activities like NREGA, IAY, Midday meal ,Old age pension, Pulse polio, Widow pension ,PH and Kutirjyoti .there are 9 households out of this NREGA gets more facilities that is 100% and here the PH and Widow Pension is nil.

Main Findings

1. The field area is mainly Schedule Tribe dominated area.
2. Education condition of the field area which is poor, so the family members cannot support to their child in education background.

3. They cannot go for higher education because and economic condition is poor.
4. Field area has less illiteracy percentage.
5. More members in family are turned to the APL.
6. Most of the families are bamboo house.
7. Most of the house roofs of families are made in straw.
8. The APL family's getting electricity more than BPL.
9. The temporary toilet higher than permanent.
10. Most of the family livestock is hen.
11. The adult male is more than adult female and also male child is more than female child.
12. The family income of Antordaya is higher than Annapurna, income of Antordaya family is less than BPL, and obviously APL families' income is much higher than the BPL families.
13. Most of the families are getting NREGA facilities.

Institutional Services of Primary School as Mid Day Meal

The Mid-Day Meal Scheme was launched by the Ministry of Human Resource Development (Department of Education) with effect from 15th August, 1995 for the benefit of students in primary schools under Employment Assurance Scheme (EAS) earlier Revamped Public Distribution System (RPDS) blocks (2368). The Scheme covers students of Class I-V in the Government Primary Schools/Primary Schools aided by Govt. and the Primary Schools run by local bodies.

Food grains (wheat and rice) are supplied free of cost @ 100 gram per child per school day where cooked/processed hot meal is being served with a Minimum content of 300 calories and 8-12 gms of protein each day of school for a minimum of 200 days and 3 kgs per student per month for 9-11 months in a year, where food grains are distributed in raw form. In drought affected areas the mid day meal is distributed in summer vacations also.

To cut down delays in implementation of the scheme, Department of Elementary Education & Literacy has been authorized to make State/DT-wise allocation of food grains under intimation to this Department. Food Corporation of India (FCI) releases food grains to States/UTs at BPL rates as per allocation made by Department of Elementary Education and Literacy.

Allocation/off take of food grains under the scheme during 2001-2002, 2002-03, 2003-04, 2004-05, 2005-06 and 2006-07 is as under:-

Table 5.88: Allocation off-take (lakh tonnes)

Year	*Rice*	*Wheat*	*Total*	*Rice*	*Wheat*	*Total*
2001-02	18.67	9.96	28.63	13.48	7.28	20.76
2002-03	18.84	9.40	28.24	13.75	7.45	21.20
2003-04	17.72	9.08	26.80	13.49	7.20	20.69
2004-05	20.14	7.35	27.49	15.41	5.92	21.33
2005-06	17.78	4.72	22.50	13.64	3.63	17.27
2006-07	17.17	4.17	21.34	10.48	2.85	13.33
						(up to January, 07)

* Annual Allocation.

Scheme for Supply of Food grains to Hostels/Welfare Institutions (5% Of BPL Allocation)

With a view to meet the requirement of Hostels welfare Institutions viz. N.G.Os Charitable Institutions, which help the homeless poor and other categories not covered under TPDS or under any other Welfare Schemes, an additional allocation of food grains (rice and wheat) equal to 5% of the BPL allocation of each State jut is made to States juts at BPL rates. This scheme was introduced during 2002-03.

Allocation/off take of food grains under the scheme during 2002-03, 2003-04, 2004-05 & 2005-06 (unto June, 2005) is as under: -

Figures in lakh tonnes

Allocation Offtake

Year	*Rice*	*Wheat*	*Total*	*Rice*	*Wheat*	*Total*
2002-03	6.58	4.53	11.11	1.30	0.14	1.44
2003-04	6.25	5.19	11.44	3.15	0.23	3.38
2004-05	6.06	4.80	10.86	1.94	0.75	2.69

2005-06	1.98	1.43 (upto June 2005)	3.41	0.27	0.05	0.32 (upto May, 2005)

Note:- offtake figure during 2002-03 & 2003-04 includes lifting against SC/ST/OBC Scheme.

Mid-Day Meal Programme in Tripura

Mid-Day Meal Programme is another flagship scheme that has been taken up by Tripura. Mid-day meals do not contain only khichuri, a mixture of boiled rice and dal but children in Agartala have a meal with egg-curry, vegetable and khichari for two days in a week. This arrangement under universalized Mid-Day Meal Programme will come up in all primary schools in Tripura soon.

About 6 lakh school children come under this programme. In 2005-06 a total of 5226 educational institutions, besides other educational centers came under this programme. The response to this programme has been tremendous.

Attendance of children from the poverty-ridden families in school has gone up and is expected to go up.

In order to achieve cent percent success and to make all children unto 14 years healthy the Government of Tripura has constituted monitoring cells involving the Panchayats. In the base level, the programme is being supervised by the cells under respective Nagar Panchayat and Gram Panchayat. Teachers and mother committees have been formed in all schools to supervise the process of cooking and distribution. State has also decided to reward best mother under this programmed.

The state govt. of Tripura launched mid-day meal scheme in the state w.e.f. 1st March, 1980 for children reading from class I-V in govt.-aided schools. Under the scheme the school going children were provided dried food like biscuits, chiru, muri and local available season fruits for 200 days in a year. Subsequently govt. of India introduced mid-day meal programmed under the scheme entitled "national programme of nutritional support to primary education" (NP-NSPE) w.e.f. 15th August 1995 in the whole country as a centrally sponsored scheme. As per guideline of the scheme, each child I-V having attendance in schools, up to 80% was supplied 3 KG of rice per month. Government of India would provide rice free of cost and Rs 50 per quintal of rice to meet transport cost of rice as central assistance.

Again in pursuance of direction of Hon' Supreme Court of India, the stele govt. begin to provide cooked meal *(khichuri)* to eligible primary school children on all school day since 1st April 2003 under mid-day meal scheme. The NP-NSPE scheme has been revised in 2004. And accordingly govt. of India has stalled providing central I assistance to all sate govt. @Rs 1 per children per school per day w.e.f 1st September. The programme of mid-day meal has been extended to all EGS &.AIE centers established under SSA scheme w.e.f. 1st Dec. 2004 in the state.

SUBJECT:- GUIDELINES IN CONNECTION WITH SUPPLY OF COOKED MEALS TO ALL CHILDREN (CLASSES I-V) OF GOVERNMENT AND GOVERNMENT AIDED PRIMARY SCHOOLS INCLUDING GOVT.AIDED MADRASSAS UNDER THE MID-DAY-MEAL (NP-NSPL) PROGRAMME WITH EFFECT FROM 1ST APRIL, 2003.

1. In pursuance of Government Memorandum No.F.8 (28-229)-DSE/2002 dated 20-12-2002 Cooked Meals (Khichudi) will be supplied under the Mid-day-meal (NP-NSPE) Programme all over the state to all children of classes I-V reading in the Government and Government aided Primary Schools/Jr. Madrassas as well as primary sections attached to all S,B., High and H.S. Schools, Senior Madrassas,as Education Guaramee Scheme (EGS) center, Alternative & Innovative Education centers with effect from 1st day of April, 2003.
2. The cooked meals *(Khichudi)* to be supplied should have a minimum content of 300 (three hundred) Calories and 8-12 grams of Protein each day of school.
3. *Khichudi* shall be prepared with rice, potato, Vegetables etc. with the quantity & cost appended below:-

Sl.No.	*Commodity.*	*Quantity.*	*Cost.*
i)	Rice.	100Gms.	Free.
ii)	Dal	25Gms	Rs.0.75
iii)	Vegetables, Fuel, Oil etc.	_	Rs.0.30
iv)	Overhead charges for carrying rice per child per day.	-	Rs.0.05
v)	Wages for cook per child per day.	-	Rs.0.10

4. The unit cost for feeding per child per day is fixed at Rs. 1.20. This apart an amount of Rs.1000 (Rupees one thousand) only shall be made available to each school as one time grant for purchase of utensils required for the purpose.
5. The programme will be implemented by the Panchayats or their authorized representatives in non-ADC and the constituted Village Development Committee in the ADC areas. Repured NGOs wherever available may also be engaged for the purpose. In Municipal Council/Nagar Panchayat areas similar Action will be taken by the respective Ward Commissioner/Ward Member of Nagar Panchayat. Panchayat or the constituted Village Development Committee (VDC) will engage 1 (one) person as Organizer who will be responsible for overall management of the programme upto actual supply of cooked meals (Khichudi) to the eligible children. In case of Municipal council and Nagar Panchayat areas the respective Municipal Ward Commissioner/Ward Member of Nagar Panchayat shall engage organizer for each school for supply of Khichudi under the above programme.
6. The food grains will be supplied by the state Food, Civil Super lies and Consumer Affairs Department through their F.P. shop dealer located nearest to the concerned school. The food grains will be lifted by the engaged organizer from the F.P. shop on production of the enrolment figure duty certified by the Headmaster of Teacher-in-charge of the concerned school/Madrassas. While lifting of food grains for the subsequent months the balance stock of rice in hand should be taker into account at the aim of

submission of requirement of food grains to the inspector of school by the HM/Teacher-in-charge.

7. One F.P. shop will be selected by the Headmaster/ Teacher-in-charge nearest to the school for lifting of food grains.
8. Fund form implementation of the programme will be placed from the School Education Directorate @ Rs.1.20 per day eligible student with concerned Inspector of schools in respect of schools under State Government including the attached primary section of High/HS schools under the territorial jurisdiction of the inspector of schools. Fund in respect of all primary schemes in ADC areas shall also be placed with the Inspector of Schools (State) in the concerned area. The Inspector of schools shall disburse the fund in advance strictly on the basis of roll strength to the Village Education Committee (V.E.C.) who will give is to the engaged Organizer.
9. The Organizer shall have to maintain the following records:-
   a) Feeding Register.
   b) Stock Register.
   c) Cash Book and Register for maintaining voucher.
10. Utmost care has to be taken about general cleanliness in regard to storage, preparation and distribution of Khichudi to children. Adequate care has also to be taken about provision of drinking water.
11. Attendance of students in the register will be marked as "P" to denote present and "A" to denote absent by the school authorities. No absence will be marked as dot (.).
12. The HM/Teacher-in-charge shall maintain a separate grant and feeding registers and statements pertaining to utilization of food grains and grants for the programme.
13. One time grant to the extent of Rs. 1000/- for procuring utensils, deceit, data, bucket, drum for storing water will be given to each school by the

concerned inspector of Schools. The Headmaster/teacher-in-charge will purchase those articles in consultation with the Mother-Teacher Association.

14. On each feeding day the Headmaster/Teacher-in-charge immediately after roll call shall supply the firm figure of attendance to the organizer who will prepare food (Khichudi) based on the attendance of children as received from the H.M. or Teacher-in-charge of the school.
15. At the end of each month the organizers shall finalize the accounts of expenditure and submit the same to the Headmaster/Teacher-in-charge of the concerned school only certified by the pradhan of the pachayat or Chairman of the concerned Village Development Committee. In case of the Nagar Panchayat and Municipal areas the accounts are to be certified by the Ward Commissioner or ward member as the case may be. Headmaster/Teacher-in-charge shall furnish the statement of expenditure to the concerned Inspector of schools. The entire exercise is to be completed within 3rd working day of the following month.
16. The Inspector of schools shall receive reports of statement of expenditure in respect of all schools under his territorial jurisdiction including ADC and compile the same at the block level. The compiled statement of expenditure in respect of the entire block shall be submitted to the District Education officer by the 7th working day of the following month.
17. District Education Officer shall furnish the expenditure statement in respect of their respective district to the Director of School Education, Mid-Day-Meal section by the 10th working day of the following month.

MONITORING, SUPERVISION PREVIEW

18. In order to develop strong linkage between the concerned department through an institutional mechanism and for better supervision, monitoring and review of implementation of the scheme, a state

level committee will be constituted with the following members.

1.	Commissioner & Secretary Education Department.	Chairman
2.	Chief Executive Officer T.T.A.A.D.C.	Member
3.	Director Tribal Welfare Department	Member
4.	Director S.C. Welfare Department	Member
5.	Director Food, Civil Supplies & Consumer Affairs Department	Member
6.	Director Health & Family Welfare Department	Member
7.	Director, school education	Member-Secratary
8.	Director, Social Welfare & Social Education Department	Member

Similarly, District and Sub-division level committees will also be constituted of effective supervision and monitoring of the scheme with the following members.

DIST. LEVEL COMMITTEE.

1.	District Magistrate & Collector	Chairman
2.	Secretary, Zilla Parishad	Member
3.	Local M.L.A(s)	Member
4.	Zonal Development Officer, ADC	Member
5.	Representative of Nagar Panchayat	Member
6.	Dist. Inspector of Social Welfare & Social Education.	Member
7.	Chief Medical Officer.	Member
8.	District Education Officer/Deputy Director of Education.	Member-Secretary

Sub-Divisional Committee.

1.	Sub-Divisional Magistrate	Chairman
2.	All Inspector of Schools in the Sub-Division including ADC	Member
3.	Representative of Nagar Panchayat	Member
4.	Chair-Person, All Panchayat Samity	Member
5.	Assistant Director, Food	Member
6.	The Inspector of Schools in the Sub-divisional Headquarter.	Member Secretary

Village Level Committee

The existing Village Education Committees shall act as village Level Committees for the purpose.

School Level Committee

The existing Mother Teacher Association of each school shall act as School Level Committee for the purpose.

Implementation of National Programme of Nutritional support to primary Education-supply of cooked meals to all children of govt. and Govt. aided Primary schools with effect from 1st April, 2003.

1. The Government of Tripura was implementing Mid-day-Meal Programme in the state from the year 1980 covering all children of Govt. and Govt. aided Primary Schools and also primary sections attached to upper Primary, High and H.S. Schools supplying dry food like Biscuits, puffed Rice, gur and bananas etc.
2. This programme was subsequently replaced from August 15, 1995 by introducing national programme of Nutritional Support to primary Education under which rice 3Kgs per child is being supplied free of cose to the eligible children through out the state and the programme is continuing mill now in all Govt. aided primary schools including state Govt. aided primary including state Govt. aided Madrassas.

presence at the time of preparation and serving Mid-day meal is felt necessary for effective daily monitoring.

2. Therefore, it has been decided that all H/Ms and Teacher-in-charge of jr. B. Schools and S.B. High and H/S Schools having attached primary sections will prepare list of mothers of enrolled children in primary stage in their respective schools in a separate registered issue written request letter two mothers to remain present at school in turn on each school day at the time of preparation and serving of Mid-day-meal to ensure regularity and quality of the meal served the children under the programme.

Hosting Sammelen of Mother on Intimational Woman's Day in all Schools to sensitize mothers on Mid-Day-Meal Scheme-reg.

(i) All Inspector of schools both under state and TTAADC will ensure observance of international woman's Day on 08/03/06 by organizing mother sammelan in a benefiting manner in all schools and EGS centers where Mid-Day-Meal scheme are in operation under their respective control.

(ii) All Teaching staff and school children, all mothers representative of PRI'S and local dignitaries may be requested to participate in the programme to make it grand success.

(iii) Action taken report with a brief report may be submitted to this end by all Inspector of schools.

Enhancement of conversion cost from Rs 1.20 to Rs 1.50

needs revision for providing cooked food of satisfactory quality because of price hike of the articles. The matter has been carefully examined and reviewed at the appropriate level by the Department (School) of Education keeping the facts mentioned above in view.

Considering the facts as indicated above, now it has been decided to enhance the present rate of conversion cost of Rs.1.20 toRs.1.50 per child per school day w.e.f.1st day of July.2005.

Detaiked break-up of the conversion cost at the enchanced rate of 1.50 per day indicated below.

Sl. No.	*Commodities*	*Quantity*	*Cost*
1.	Rice	100Grams	Free of cost.
2.	Dal	25Grams	Rs.0.75.
3.	Vegetable, Oil fuel etc .	-	Rs.0.50.
4.	Overhead dharges for carrying Rice, Dal etc from F.P. Shop to school	-	Rs.0.05.
5.	Wages for cooking	-	Rs.0.20
	Total		Rs.1.50.

It has been reported that in some schools cooked meal (Khichudi) is not being provided to school children during Examination period which is clear violation of Hon'ble Supreme Court's order.

In the Hon'ble Supreme Court's order it is categorically mention that cooked meals must be provided to all eligible children of primary stage of all Govt. and govt. aided schools on all schools days for miniterium 200 days in a academic year.

Now, once [illegible] is reiterate[illegible] t[illegible]t servin[illegible] [illegible]d-d[illegible] Meal

We all are aware that with above reference coocked meal *(Khichudi)* will be supplied under the Mid-day-meal (NP-NSPE) over the sub-division, Sonamura to all children of class I-V reading in the Government and Government aided Primary school / Jr. Madrassa as well as primary section attached to all Sr. B. High and H.S. school Sr. Madrassa including A.D.C. schools with effect by 1st April 2003.

In this connection every school under Mid-day-Meal programme will get is.1,000/- (Rupees One thousand) only in one time grant for purchase of utincel required for the purpose and cost of preparation of cooked meal from Education Inspectorate, Sonamura (State) within the 25th March,2005. The organizer of every school appointed by Gram panchayet will supply the khichudi prepared the them. If no organizer is apponted in any school the H.M/T.I.C. must provide Mid day Meal w.e.f.1st April 2003.

For fullness of above mentioned programme the all H.M/ T.I.C. of every school under jurisdiction of Sonamura Sub-Division including TTADC are cordially requested to draw the all grants for supplying the cooked to your own school within the 25th March 2003 without any delay and at the time of receipt of the same all are requested to conduct the meeting with Dy.I.S, Sonamura and Kathalia, Boxanagar Block positively.

This is treated as top most Urgent.

Enchancement of cooking cost norm and nutritional norm under Mid-day-Meal programme

1. In supersession of all previous orders, now it has been decided to enhance the existing cooking cost norm of Rs.1.50 to Rs.2.30 per child per day under NP-NSPE (Mid-day-meal) programme w.e.f.1st September 2006. Accordingly, the nutritional norm has also been raised to minimum 450 calories and 12 grams of protein. This decision has been taken in view of enhancement of central assistance from existing Rs. 1.00 to Rs 1.80 per child per day towards cooking cost by Govt. of India w.e.f.16.06.2006. The state will continue Rs.0.05 per child per day.

2. As the cooking cost norm as well as the nutritional norm have been revised in order to improve the quality of mid-day-meal and make the recine more palatable, it has been further decided to revise the existing weekly menu as follows.

i). Khichudi:- Twice in a week

ii). Rice, dal and vegetable:- Twice in a week

iii). Rice and egg curry- Twice in a week

3. Details of cooking cost norm for the above weekly menu are given below:-

For Khichudi and Rice, dal and vegetable curry:-

Sl.No.	*Item*	*Quantity*	*Cost*	*Calories value in KCL*	*Protein Content (in grams)*
1.	Food grain (Rice)	100gm	Free of cost	340	8
2.	Pulse (Dal)	25 gm	Rs.1.00	86	-
3.	Vegetables leafy & others	50gm	Rs.0.50	25	6.27gm
4.	Oil	5gm	Rs.0.25	45	-
5.	Overhead charges for carrying rice per child per day.	-	Rs0.05	-	-
6.	Wages for cooks per child per day.	-	Rs.0.20	-	-
7.	Fuel	-	Rs.0.10	-	-
8.	Salt & Condiments as per needs.	-	Rs.0.10	-	-
9.	Contingences for organizer-		Rs.0.10	-	-
	Total		Rs.2.30	496	14.27

Sl No.	*Item*	*Quantity*	*Cost*	*Calories value in KCL*	*Protein Content (in grams)*
1.	Food grain (rice)	100gm	Free of cost	5	6
1.	Egg	60gm	Rs.1.90	340	8
2.	Vegetables leafy & others		Rs.0.05	104	8gm
4.	Oil, fuel, salt etc.	-	Rs.0.05		
5.	Overhead charges for carrying rice per child per day	-	Rs.0.05	45	-
6.	Wages of cooks per child per day	-	Rs. 0.20	-	-
7.	Contingencies for organizer		Rs. 0.20	-	-
	Total		Rs 2.30	489	16

Weekly menu and its Nutritional assessment:

Weekly menu for Mid-day meal programme has been prepared by a three member committee constituted with a dietician, nutritionist and a Joint Director in the state, while preparing the menu, they have properly assessed the food values of each item included in the item. The quality of food and its nutritional values are being ensured through effective supervision by the MTA at school level on daily basis.

Organizational chart and Administrative costing:

In Tripura school education in the nodal department of implementation of Mid-day meal Programme and director of school in the state nodal officer. At the director of school education, a Mid-day meal cell has been created to assist the state nodal officer for proper management of implementation of the scheme. Similarly at the district and block level offices there are Mid-day meal cells with provision of staff. The Mid-day meal cells is headed by a Joint Director at the state level by a district level office at the district level and by a Deputy Inspector of the block level officers

Required posts of clerical and Deputy Inspector of Schools were created under Mid day meal scheme when it was first started in the state in the early 80s and now the cost on account of salaries of these staffs are being borne under non plan heads in the state annual budget. At the Sub-Block level there are circle officers headed by Deputy Inspectors who are supervising the scheme. At the school level the head teachers look after the Mid-day meal programme.

Table 5.89: Average attendance (%)

SL. No	*Percentage (%)*
School-1	96.00
School-2	82.00
School-3	75.90
School-4	90.00
School-5	81.96
School-6	90.00
School-7	85.00

Source: Field Survey, 2007.

From the above table it is clear that in school-1 there is highest Average attendance and school-3 there is lowest average attendance.

Although this percentage is more high after implementation of Mid-day meal. No register khata is found to take data of attendance before launching Mid-day meal. It is the constraint of study.

Table 5.90: Facilities available in school

Library facility

Library	*No. of School*	*Percentage(%)*
Yes	-	-
No	7	100
Total	7	100

Source: Field Survey-2007.

The above table shows that number of school having library facility, library is the backbone of any academic institution, which provide new concept, ideas knowledge to the students / readers, but it is the lacuna in these all schools whose students are deprived from library.

Table 5.91: Table-Reading room facility

Reading room	*No. of School*	*Percentage(%)*
Yes	-	-
No	7	100
Total	7	100

Source: Field Survey, 2007.

The above table reveals that the reading room facility is not available in surveyed school.

As there is no Reading room facility in the school library, the students faced disturbance and concentrate on their study thus the effect is not good.

Table 5.92: Playground facility

Playground	*No. of School*	*Percentage (%)*
Yes	5	71.42
No	2	28.57
Total	7	100

Source: Field Survey, 2007.

The above table depicts that 71.42% school has playground facilities. On the other hand 28.57% of school has no any play ground.

In 28.57% of school has no playground facility because the area of the school is short and school is situated beside the road.

Table 5.93: Safe Drinking Water

Safe drinking water	*No. of School*	*Percentage (%)*
Yes	2	28.57
No	5	71.42
Total	7	100

Source: Field Survey, 2007.

The above table shows that 28.57% school has safe drinking water facilities. On the other hand 71.42% school has no safe drinking water facilities.

So we can say that much more school has terrible condition or poor condition in safe drinking water.

Table 5.94: Separate Toilet for Boys and Girls

Separate toilet for boys and girls	*No. of School*	*Percentage (%)*
Yes	3	42.85
No	4	57.14
Total	7	100

Source: Field Survey, 2007.

The above table shows that, 42.85% of school has separate toilet for boys and girls. On the other hand 57.14% of school has not separate toilet for boys and girls.

In those school where have no separate toilet for boys and girls thus the children practice open deification. So it creates disturbances of school environment.

Table 5.95: Present status of Student's Health

Present status of students health	*No. of school*	*Percentage (%)*
Most of them are healthy students	-	-
Average	7	100
Most of them are poor health	-	-
Mal nutrition's	-	-
Total	7	100

Source: Field Survey, 2007.

The above table shows that, health condition of the school going student under class (I-V) are average.

Average means neither they are healthy or nor they are poor in health condition.

Mid-day meal helps the students to maintaining average health; Mid-day programme provides nutritious food in everyday like vegetable, egg etc.

Table 5.96: Separate kitchen

Separate kitchen	*No. of School*	*Percentage(%)*
Yes	6	85.71
No	1	14.28
Total	7	100

Source: Field Survey, 2007.

Table 5.97: Items provided to the Student

Items provided to the student	*No. of days (weekly)*	*Percentage (%)*
Rice	4	66.66
Dal	2	33.33
Meat	-	-
Egg	2	33.33
Green leafy, vegetables	2	33.33
Khichuri	2	33.33
Others	-	-
Total	6 days	-

The above tables reveal that most schools having separate kitchen facility which is 85.71% and only 14.28% have no separate kitchen.

So it can be said, that the class room is more hygienic students are not disturbed by smoke or any hazards.

Table 5.98: Who cook the meal?

Cook the meal	*No. of school*	*Percentage (%)*
SHGs	2	28.57
Organizer	5	71.42
NGOs	-	-
Total	7	100

Source: Field Survey, 2007.

The above table reveals that most of the cooks are organise, these organizers are involved by panchayat, where as less percentage of cook are SHG members, the SHG member give good service to the school but organizer creates many problems.

So it can be said, that the SHG members should be involved more in this work, because they are the good service provider regularly to mid-day meals.

The above depicts that, the items which provide to the student as Mid-day meal that is 66.66% of rice in a week and the other items like dal, egg, green leaf vegetables, khichuri as 33.33 respectively.

So it is the clear that most of the students prefer to take rice and egg because it is delicious food.

No. of dropout class I-V (present)

All the surveyed school present number of dropout is nil (after launching Mid-day meal)

It is the good effect of Mid-day meal that present condition of dropout is nil and other wise it is the nutritious food.

Table 5.99: Previous dropout rate (before launching Mid-day meal)

Dropout class wise	*Previous dropout*	*Percentage*
Class-I	1	4.76
Class-II	4	19.04
Class-III	3	14.28
Class-IV	4	19.04

Class-V	9	42.85
Total	21	100

Source: Field survey, 2007.

Before launching Mid-day meal programme the dropout rate was high in class-V and the dropout was in class-I.

So it can be said that Mid-day meal is not responsible for the dropout of class-V students there are other reasons having balanced this dropout

Table 5.100: Difference in attendance before and after launching Mid-day meal

SL. No	*Before attendance (%)*	*After attendance Percentage (%)*
School-1	70.00	96.00
School-2	60.00	82.00
School-3	70.00	75.90
School-4	65.00	90.00
School-5	75.00	81.96
School-6	55.00	90.00
School-7	62.00	85.00

Source: Field Survey, 2007.

The above table shows that, before launching Mid-day meal the attendance is higher in school -3 that is 72.00% and the lowest in school-6 that is 55.00% on the other hand, from the above table it is clear that after launching Mid-day meal attendance is higher in school-1 that is 96.00% and the lowest attendance in school-3 that is 75.00% .

So it is the good effect of Mid-day meal. Parents think that his child will get food fulfill for the stomach if he goes to school, only for this reasons every students come to school.

Major problems of running the Mid-day meal (*Source*: - Field survey, 2007)

(i) Lack of safe drinking water. (Filtering)

(ii) It is the rule to provide utensils to the every students but they did' not get.

(iii) Only one person is engaged in Mid-day meal, no extra helper serving the food.

(iv) Lack of storage facility (Rice)

(v) Most of the surveyed school no separate kitchen for Mid-day meal, it is close to classroom.

(vi) Food items rate is not enough which is lower than market rate.

(vii) Fuel cost is very low.

(viii) Rice is not good quality.

Table 5.101: Balanced nutrition from Mid-day meal

Sl. No	*No. of school balance nutrition*	*Percentage (%)*
Yes	5	71.42
No	2	28.57
Total	7	100

Source: Field survey, 2007.

It is the above narrates that most of the school going children balanced nutritions food only 28.57% doesn't give balanced food.

Where the SHG members are engaged as cook, the quality of food is very good because they have taken the all responsibility including marketing catering etc, the mother of the students are the members of this SHGs.

Again the schools, where balanced food is not given there the organizer are engaged as cook, they are involved in malpractices only for this reason, and the students are deprived from good quality food. It can be mentioned that organizer are engaged by the panchayat no mother are involved.

Suggestions to improve Mid-day meal (Teacher)

These are-

(i) Providing safe drinking water facility (filtering)

(ii) Mid-day meal cooking purpose fuel cost increase.(LPG)

(iii) Providing good quality of good items.

(iv) Every school should utensils to the every student.

(v) Employed extra worker for cooking purpose in every school.

(vi) In every school separate toilet for boys & girls must be created.

(vii) The distance of kitchen room must be far away from class room.

(viii) Proper storage facility is needed for rice, dal etc.

(ix) It is necessary that everyday at least two mothers are attend in school to look after the quality of meal.

Table 5.102: Involvement of SHG/NGO/Organizer

Involvement	*No. of School*	*Percentage (%)*
SHG	2	28.57
NGO	-	-
Organizer	5	71.42
Total	7	100

Source: Field survey, 2007.

The above table shows that, the cooking of mid-day meal by organizer is 71.42%. On the other hand only 28.57% of school cook khichuri by SHG members.

Cooks are engaged by Gram Panchayat (SHGs / Organizer) are responsible for cooking Mid-day meal.

Table 5.103: Contact any meeting with parents about Mid-day meal

Parents meeting about Mid-day meal	*No. of school*	*Percentage*
Yes	7	100
No	-	-
Total	7	100

Source: Field survey, 2007.

All the surveyed school contact M.T.A. (Mother Teacher Association) committee, with parents about Mid-day meal

Head teacher opinion that, Mother Teacher Association committee and two mothers on each day supervise the proparation of meal and ensure use of specified qualify of rice, dal & other seasonal vegetables on daily basis in all schools.

Join in this profession (Mid-day meal worker)

Ist April 2003 worker engaged in this profession. The

organizer or helper is not being paid. They are rendering voluntary service. The cooks are being paid Re. 0.20 per child.

Table 5.104: Wash the vegetables properly before cooking

Wash the vegetable	*No. of school*	*Percentage*
Yes	7	100
No	-	-
Total	7	100

Source: Field Survey, 2007.

In all the surveyed school the worker wash the vegetables properly before cooking.

Table 5.105: Helper in cook

Cook in Gas stove	*No. of school*	*Percentage*
Yes	2	28.57
No	5	71.42
Total	7	100

Source: Field survey, 2007.

The above table narrates that 28.57% helper cook khichuri by Gas stove.

Table 5.105: Helper cook in fuel wood

Fuel wood	*No. of school*	*Percentage*
Yes	5	71.42
No	2	28.57
Total	7	100

Source: Field survey, 2007.

The above table shows that 71.42% helper cook khichuri by fuel wood.

The teacher increased that the cook use the LPG but in fact the cook do not use LPG. Earthen oven, Electric oven, cow dong, Bio gas etc are not use cooking khichuri purpose.

Table 5.106: Use clear water for cooking

Use clear water for cooking	*No. of school*	*Percentage*
Yes	7	100
No	-	-
Total	7	100

Source: Field survey, 2007.

In all the surveyed school the worker uses clear water for cooking purpose.

Table 5.107: Family size

Caste	*Small size family (1-3)*	*Percentage*	*Big size family (above) 3*	*Percentage*	*G.T.*
SC	5	45.45	12	30.76	17
ST	2	18.18	6	15.38	8
OBC	3	27.27	16	41.02	19
GEN	I	9.09	5	12.82	6
Total	II	100	39	100	50

Source: Field survey, 2007.

The above table shows that 45.45% of SC population belongs in small size family that is highest, and the 9.09% of general population belongs in small size family. On the other hand 41.02% of OBC population belongs in size family which is the highest percentage and the 12.82% of Gen population belongs in big size family which is the lowest percentage.

Table 5.108: population according to age group

Age group	*SC*	*% of SC*	*ST*	*% of ST*	*OBC*	*% of OBC*	*GEN*	*% of GEN*	*Total*
1-5	2	2.53	-	-	1	1.17	-	-	3
5-10	3	3.79	7	20.58	17	20	4	16.66	31
10-15	9	11.39	2	5.88	3	3.52	9	37.5	23
15-20	7	8.86	-	-	12	14.11	5	20.83	24
20-25	12	15.18	9	26.47	14	16.47	-	-	35
25-30	18	22.78	3	8.82	3	3.52	2	8.33	26
30-35	13	16.45	5	14.70	16	18.82	1	4.16	35
35-40	-	-	8	23.52	7	8.23	1	4.16	16
Above 40	15	18.98	-	-	12	14.11	3	12.5	30
Total	79	100	34	100	85	100	24	100	223

Source: Field survey, 2007.

The above table shows that 22.78% of SC population belongs in 25-30 age group. Which is the highest percentage of age group on the other hand 1.17% of OBC population belongs in 1-5 age group that is the lowest percentage of age group.

Table 5.109: Education status

Education	*Population*	*Percentage*
I-V	17	28.81
VI-VIII	19	32.20
IX-X	6	10.16
XI-XII	13	22.03
B.A./B.Sc./B.Com.	3	5.08
M.A./M.Sc./M.Com.	1	1.69
Total	59	100

Source: Field survey, 2007.

The above table shows that, 28.81% of the survey population belongs to (I-V) pass group, followed by (VI-VIII) pass group is 32.20%, (IX-X) pass group is 10.16% & (XI-XII) pass group is 22.03% and the graduate & Master degree holder is 5.08% & 1.69%

Table 5.110: Drop out scenario

Caste	*Male*	*% of Male*	*Female*	*% of Female*	*Total*
SC	7	77.77	2	22.22	9
ST	-	-	-	-	-
OBC	-	-	-	-	-
GEN	-	-	-	-	-

Source: Field Survey, 2007.

The above table analyses that, I child are found dropout from the primary education, among with 77.77%, of total dropout children are male & 22.22% children are female.

Table 5.111: Main occupation

Main occupation	*Population*	*Percentage*
Agriculture	15	21.12
Daily labour	7	9.85
Catching & selling fish	29	40.84
Bamboo wook	9	12.67
Fisheries	7	9.85
Service	3	4.22
Business	1	1.40
Total	71	100

Source: Field survey, 2007.

The above table narrates that, most of the people 40.84% of the earned population's main occupation is catching & selling fish & 21.12% of the earned people have a main occupation as agriculture labour.

Table 5.112: Family Expenditure

	No. of Family							
Family expenditure (Monthly)	*SC*	*% of SC*	*ST*	*% of ST*	*OBC*	*% of OBC*	*GEN*	*% of GEN*
Rs. up to 1500	7	41.17	3	37.5	6	31.57	-	-
Rs. 1500-3000	3	17.64	-	-	3	15.78	4	66.66
Rs. 3001-4500	5	29.41	5	62.5	3	15.78	-	-
Rs. 4501-5500	2	11.76	-	-	7	36.84	2	33.33
Above Rs. 5500	-	-	-	-	-	-	-	-
Total	17	100	8	100	19	100	6	100

Source: Field survey, 2007.

The above table shows that, the most of the No. of family monthly expenditure SC families is 41.17% (Rs. up to 1500.)ST families 62.5% is between Rs. 3001-4500, OBC families is 36.84% (is between Rs. 4501-5500)and GEN families is 66.6% is between Rs. 4501-5500.

Table 5.113: Disease Prevail in the study area

Disease	*No. of population*	*Percentage*
Stomachache	2	15.38
Fever	6	46.15
Small pox	-	-
Bronchitis Amashaya	2	15.38
Amashaya	-	-
Diarrhoea	3	23.07
Total	13	100

Source: Field survey, 2007.

The above table revels that, 46.15% population effected by fiver diseases and most of the population effected by different diseases like as stomach ache, bronchitis, Diarrhea.

Table 5.113: Source of Drinking water

Source	*Family*	*Percentage*
Tube well	34	68
Dip Tube well	7	14
Tube well + Dip Tube well	5	10
Well water	4	8
Total	50	100

Source: Field survey, 2007.

The above table shows that, 68% of the families are using tube well a source of drinking 14% of the families are using Dip tube well & 10% of the total families are gating the facilities of both tube well and Dip tube well. And the 8% of the total families are using tube well a source of drinking.

Table 5.113: Electric Connections

Electric connection	*Family*	*Percentage*
Yes	29	58
No	21	42
Total	50	100

Source: Field survey, 2007.

The above table shows that, 58% of the total families are facilitated by electric connection.

Ration card

All the surveyed families have access of the Ration Card. (*Source:* Field survey, 2007)

Table 5.114: House Type

House type	*Family*	*Percentage*
Kancha	24	48
Brick	3	6
Half wall	7	14
Bamboo made house	16	32
Total	50	100

Source: Field survey, 2007.

The above tabe shows the 48% of the families houses are 'Kancha'. And 6% of the families houses are Brick, and 32% of the families have 'Bamboo made house.

Table 5.115: Livestock

Live stock	*No. of families*	*Percentage*
Cattle	9	30
Goats	12	40
Sheep	-	-
Poultry	-	-
Pig	6	20
Duck	3	10
None	-	-
Total	30	100

Source: Field survey, 2007.

The above table clear that, 40% families have goats and 10% families have duck.

Table 5.116: Status of school going children

Health status	*No. of families*	*Percentage*
Good	12	24
Average	31	62
Poor	7	14
Total	50	100

Source: Field survey, 2007.

The above table reveals that, 62% families children's health status is average, and 14% families' children's health status is poor.

Average means neither good health nor bad health.

Table 5.117: Availability of food

Take enough food	*No. of families*	*Percentage*
Yes	35	70
No	15	30
Total	50	100

Source: Field survey, 2007.

The above table narrates that, 70% families child take enough food.

Table 5.117: Children's attendance

Regularly school going	*No. of Families*	*Percentage*
Yes	50	100
No	-	-
Total	50	100

Source: Field survey, 2007.

All the surveyed families' children go school regularly.

Table 5.118: Regularity of children

Regularly going to School	*No. of families*	*Percentage*
Yes	19	38
No	31	62
Total	50	100

Source: Field survey, 2007.

The above table clears that, 38% families' children going to school regularly due to mid-day meal.

Table 5.119: Other benefits of Mid-day meal

Benefits of Mid-day meal	*No. of families*	*Percentage*
Nutrition's food	13	26
Break fast food	11	22
Full stomach	26	52
Total	50	100

Source: Field survey, 2007.

The above table shows that, 52% families said that the other benefit of Mid-day meal is full stomach the children and the 26% families said that it the nutrition food.

Table 5.120: Any improvement or ill effect due to Mid-day meal

Health status	*No. of families*	*Percentage*
Improvement in appetite.	22	44
Ill effect	-	-
No comments.	28	56
Total	50	100

Source: Field survey, 2007.

The above table analyses that, 44% family's children health status improvement in appetite.

Most of the families think that their children benefited from this Mid-day meal because their children get enough food in the school and after coming home they do not want food again. The family members think that it is the improvement of their children in appetite.

Suggestion for improvement of Mid-day meal (families)

The factors that can be improve Mid-day meal:

i) Providing safe drinking water facility

ii) Providing good quality of food items (Rice, Dal etc)

iii) Use clear water for cooking and cleaning utensils.

Table 5.121: Attended the Parents Meeting

Attended the parents meeting	*No. of families*	*Percentage*
Yes	39	78
No	11	22
Total	50	100

Source: Field survey, 2007.

The table revels that, 78% families attend the parents meeting, and 22% families not attend the parents meeting.

Major Findings

1. Among all the surveyed schools no registrar khata is found to take data of attendance before launching mid-day mill

2. In all the surveyed school there is no library facility and also no reading room facilities
3. Most of the surveyed school has no safe drinking water
4. Most of the school going children's health condition class I-V are average
5. 14.28% surveyed school have no separate kitchen room. It is close to class room. So it can be said that the class room is not more hygienic, students are disturbed by smoke
6. 71.42% cooks are organizers. These organizers are involved by Panchayet, where less percentage of cooks are SHG members, the SHG member give good service to the school but organizer creates many problems. So it can be said that the SHG members should be involved more in this work because they are the good service provider regarding mid-day meal
7. In most of the surveyed school only 1 person is engaged in mid-day meal. No extra helper is serving food
8. 28.57% helper cook Khichuri by gas stove and 71.42% helper cook khichuri by fuel wood. The teacher involved in fund embezzlement and thus they engage to cook by fuel wood instead of LPG.
9. Most of the families think that their children are benefited from the mid-day meal because their child get enough food in the school and after coming back home they do not want food again. The family member think that it is the improvement of their children in appetite.
10. All the surveyed school presented that no of drop out rate is nil after launching mid-day meal
11. Fuel cost of different days are different for the preparation of mid-day meal. There is a significant discrimination in fuel cost which is Rs. 0.05 for egg and vegetables and Rs. 0.10 for Khichuri, rice and vegetables.

Teacher, Parents and Students (Result & Effect)

Result/Problem	*Effect*
1. No separate class room	All students sit in a common class and they read the same subject.
2. No separate teacher's room.	Teachers use the same class room as their common room.
3. No separate Kitchan for Mid-day meal	Mid-day meal is cooked in the nearest household.
4. Having separate kitchen but it is closed to class room.	Unhygienic class room, students' apathyness in class.
5. Government provided LPG to every surveyed schools	Schools use wood/cake as fuel; they do not use LPG, because it is costly. There is a significant discrimination in fuel cost, which is Rs. 0.5 for egg & vegetable and Rs. 0.10 for khichuri, rich & vegetable.
6. <u>Confession of Head Master:</u> Whether it is Mid-day meal or Mid-day Tiffin	The quality of food items is sufficient for class-I, class – II student but unfortunately in much more in sufficient for class-III, class-V students.
7. Food items rate is not enough which is lower than market rate.	There is a shortage in providing non-vegetable items. Village people think that the head master is involved in mal practice. Head master is trying to fulfill the rest amount food items by saving fuel cost.
8. Only one person is engaged in Mid-day meal no extra person for serving the food.	Students engaged for carrying, serving the khichuri.
9. It is the rule to provide utensils to the every students, but they did not get	Quarter of the students for get to bring their own pot in the school, as a result they do not eat the Mid-day-meal, they are kept in empty stomach, the

excess of the mid-day meal is brought by the worker or the teachers consume it.

Role of Stake Holder Like Head Teacher, Gram Panchayat Member, Organizer, Village Education Committee (VEC) and Others

Head Teacher

Head Teacher who is the convener of MTA (Mother Teacher Associations) is responsible for maintaining stock book of rice and other food ingredients and accounts of receipt and expenditure of mid day meal fund

He keeps all vouchers in his custody and submit utilization of rice and fund to the inspector of schools. MTA members holds once in a month and take decision and corrective measures for effective implementation of the programme in each school.

Gram Panchayet

One organizer and required cooks are engaged for each school by the Gram Panchayet or ward committee to run the programme.

Organizer and Headmaster

The organizer receives fund from the head master on weekly basis and make expenditure of Dal, Vegetable, Oil and Spices and draws rice from the ration shop. After expenditure he submit vouchers to the Head master.

VEC (Village Education Committee)

In Tripura the VEC leaded by Pradhan of Gram Panchayet or Ward member supervise the implementation of the scheme in all schools located within their respective areas.

SIPARD

SIPARD has been selected as external agency for evaluation of the programme.

Institutional Role on Agriculture Marketing

Agriculture Marketing is a process which starts with a decision to produce a saleable form of commodity and it involves all aspects of market structure or system, both functional and institutional and includes pre and post – harvest operations assembly, grading, storage, transportation and distribution. It is necessary to improve the marketing system to old the process of agricultural development for firstly its absence will act as a disincentive to the farmer and secondiy if the production system dose not supply food grains and other agricultural commodities at reasonable prices to consumers at the time and place needed by them, increased production has no meaning in a welfare society. Elsewhere while analyzing the importance of marketable surplus in a developing economy Morris Dobb opines that "if there is any factor to be singled out as a fundamental limiting factor upon the pace of development it is the marketable surplus of agriculture, this rather then the total productivity of agriculture in general.

The adoption of scientific technology of agricultural produce by the farmers created a great demand for better and improved inputs in greater quantity. The investments in new technology largely depend upon the grains of the farming community. It has, therefore, become imperative that arrangements should exist for efficient movement of the farmers produce to the consumers and for adequate and timely supply of superior inputs to the farmers. In the dynamics of a growing agriculture economy the present marketing system which is out-moded, inadequate, and devoid of infrastructure facilities, has been serving as a serious constraint to development of agricultural sector and has resulted in uunremunerative prices to the farmers and un reasonable prices to the consumers.

The objective of all economic activities is the satisfaction of human wants. In order to achieve this objective the manufacturers, miners and farmers undertake production of goods and services. But they will fail to achieve their objective if the goods and services as produced do not reach the consumers who demand them at a time when they need them.

It is marketing when helps making goods useful to the society by getting them where they are wanted, when they are wanted and by transferring them to those people who want them marketing in this sense has been defined as "all the activities involved in the creation of place, time and possession utilities. To emphasize all there aspects of marketing, Clark and Clark wrote that, "Marketing consists of those efforts which effect transfer in ownership of goods and care for their physical distribution".

Importance of Agricultural Marketing

With the advance in the intensive cropping, processing, storage and marketing of agricultural produce are becoming more and more important. In the absence of sound marketing facilities, the farmers have to depend on local traders and middlemen for the disposal of their farm produce which is sold at throw away prices. In case if small and marginal farmers, marketing of produce is still more critical. Since the amount of produce they are able to sell is small and overhead expenditure on processing, transport and marketing of the produce is heavy, the marketing of their produce is hardly remunerative if they do it of their own. Owens and Shaw very aptly pointed out, "Agricultural development is first of all a human problem, not a technical problem. If all farmers have access to production inputs, the financial system, the market and agricultural knowledge, then they can improve the state of agriculture. But most farmers lack access to a market system and thus lack both the resources and the incentives to modernize their production methods". The authors add, "Unequal access to the market is one of the reasons why the Green Revolution in India has benefited mostly large farmers."

Thus for the development of agricultural sector, it is essential to develop agricultural marketing so as to match with the production surplus resulting from technological innovations and exploitation of the existing land and water resources. Apart from increasing production, marketing and distribution can significantly help in improving the availability of goods and services and also provide a stimulus to greater production. Had it not been for modern marketing, probably the Englishman would not have had his breakfast eggs from Denmark, Corn flakes from Canada, and a cup of tea from the East. Marketing also increases demand which will provide its own incentive to increase supply. This point can be illustrated by taking an example. Production of peas, for example, is seasonal and is limited to certain areas in the country because of the climate factors. But if national market for green peas is developed, a guaranteed price and a stable income will provide an incentive to the farmers to grow peas on a larger area.

Classification of Agricultural Marketing

(A) According to Seller
  1. Primary Market
  2. Secondary Market
  3. Terminal Market.

(B) According to Time
  1. Daily Market
  2. Short Period Market
  3. Long Period Market.

(C) According to Competition
  1. Perfect Market
  2. Imperfect Market.
  3. Monopoly Market

(D) According to Regulation
  1. Regulated Market.
  2. Un-regulated Market.

(E) According to Area
  1. Local Market.
  2. National Market.
  3. International Market.

(F) According to Function
  1. General or Mired Market.
  2. Specialized Market.

3. Marketing by Samples.
4. Marketing by Grades.

(G) According to Sale
1. Whole Sale Market.
2. Retail Market.

(H) According to Organization.
1. Organized Market.
2. Unorganized Markets.

Marketing Processes

Agricultural marketing involves, in its simplest form, the buying and selling of agricultural produce. Most Villages or clusters of villages in India have a market which assembles once or twice a week, and a transfer of small agricultural surpluses, from vegetables to grains takes place between the producer and the consumer, or to itinerant traders and commission agents. Village markets are poorly equipped. They lack storage, weighing and grading facilities. The importance of village markets varies from region to region. In modern times, the marketing of agricultural produce has become a complicated process and has assumed special importance. Figs. 1 and 2 show the widening of the size of the market for agricultural produce and the Chain of intermediaries or middlemen who constitute a market.

Market and Marketing Institutions

In the case of agriculture markets, three types can be defined: firstly, The primary or village markets known as Haat or Shandy which are about 22,000 at present in India and serve an average area of 8 -16 kilometers radius although some of the bigger markets serve a wider area. There are, at present, in the country about 4145 larger markets situated either at Tehsil headquarters or in large villages or towns. These are variously classed at present as secondary markers or wholesale markets or Assembly markets. Among the existing secondary or terminal markers 2936 i.e. 70% are regulated markers. Most of the villages have to rely on Haats and weekly markets. There are representatives of big traders who also visit villages periodically for purchase of commodities.

The second important aspect of the structure of marketing in India is concerned with the different methods of trading employed in markets. A large percentage of the sate of produce of done in the village itself. (Table –1) The most important characteristic of farm products which affect their marketing are bulk, seasonal production, perishability and variation in quality and volume from season to season. The bulk of the farm products and too many producers existing in the rural sector makes their transportation difficult and expensive. The fluctuation in the quality of the crop further complicates the matter.

Table 5.122: Production and Market Arrivals (1980 – 81)

Crop	*Production (Crore Tons)*	*Market Arrivals (Percentage)*
Paddy	5.38	27.9
Wheat	3.18	31.9
Jowar	1.14	9.8
Gram	0.34	36.3

Source: Directorate of Marketing and Inspection.

Most of the cultivators sell their produce in the villages due to the following reasons:

(i) The farmer's urgent need for cash after the harvest for making various payments compels him to sell he produce in the village.

(ii) On account of bad means of communication and lack of good roads i.e. transport difficulties a producer is compelled to sell his produce in the village.

(iii) Indebtedness and

(iv) Small size of the saleable surplus in the absence of carting facilities at cheaper cost producers does not undertake the task of taking their produce direct to the market.

The average villager is always a loser whether in purchasing or in selling. He is also not familiar with the market technique and therefore, cannot bargain as well as a professional byopari. Of late, the tendency is for the cultivator to cart his own produce to the market particularly where the roads are good and where he has his own means of conveyance. It is to be noted that the cultivator is not so simple minded or ignorant as he is often depicted to be. The U.P. Provincial enquiry Committee observed: "It is not, however, true that the Mahajan (Initial Investor) or Beopari can always get the cultivator into his grip or that he abuses his advantage. The cultivators are shrewd enough to ascertain the mandi prices and to calculate their transport and other purchases; and the solvent among them often dispose of their produce not to the beopari but directly at the mandi."

Defects of Agricultural Marketing

The major defects of the agricultural marketing system are outlined below:

a) Distress Sales

The Indian farmer's has to sell off his produce immediately after the harvest. Therefore, there sales are virtually distress sales either in the villages primary market on to the local money tender.

b) Lack of Storage Facilities

The Storage Facilities available with farmers in the form of pits on katcha stone houses, Kothis, etc. are inadequate to protect their crops over a fairly long period of time from dampers and other vermin's like ants, rats etc.

c) Malpractices of Middlemen in Mandis

The cultivators make use of the services of a broken to sell his output to the big wholesaler. The price which is settled is generally to the advantage of the arhatiya and not the farmer.

d) Inadequate and Expensive Means of Transport

The distress sales are further facilitated by the fact that the means of transportation available to the farmers are inadequate and for from satisfactory.

e) Lack of Grading and Standardization

The other factor that makes things difficult for the farmer is the absence of proper grading and standardization of agricultural product.

Barabhiya Gram Panchayat at a Glance (Village-I)

1.	Total boundary of the Panchayat	:	18 km.
2.	Total agricultural Land	:	400 ha.
3.	Total number of families	:	891
	(a) O.B.C.	:	589 (%)
	(b) S.C.	:	98
	(c) Minority	:	62
	(d) Others	:	142
4.	Total Population	:	8574
	(a) Male Population	:	2355
	(b) Female Population	:	2219
	Sex ratio:		
	Occupational Status		
1.	E.P.L. Card holder	:	236
2.	Antodaya Card Holder	:	144
3.	A.P.L. Card Holder	:	511
4.	Total number of families with Agricultural occupation	:	261
5.	Small Businessman	:	75
6.	Govt. Employee	:	145
	Different Govt. Officer/Institutions		
1.	Primary School	:	03
2.	High School	:	01
3.	I.C.D.S.	:	05
4.	Panchayat Office	:	01
5.	Forest Office	:	01
6.	Agriculture Sector Office	:	01
7.	Sub. Health Centre	:	01

8.	Veterinary Hospital	:	01
9.	Gramin Bank	:	01
10.	Post Office	:	01
11.	Ration Shop	:	01
12.	Electric Office	:	01
13.	Electric Line	:	8.5 Km
	Source of Irrigation		
1.	L.I. Scheme	:	02
2.	Deep tube-well	:	01
	Road Communication		
1.	Pucca Road	:	5.5 KM
2.	Brick Soaling Road	:	7 Km
3.	Katcha Road	:	17 Km
	Source of Drinking Water		
1.	Deep Tube-Well	:	02
2.	Sanitary Well	:	12
3.	Machinery Well	:	04
4.	Mud–Well	:	38
5.	Mark – 2/3	:	20
6.	Supply Water Point	:	65

Source: Barabhiaya Gram Panchayat Office.

Socio-Economic features of Chhataria Gram Panchayat (Village – II)

Chhataria Gram Panchayat at a Glance:

1.	Total Area	:	4 Sq. km.
2.	Total Agricultural Land	:	139.68 ha
3.	Total Population	:	3015
	(a) O.B.C.	:	511
	(b) S.C.	:	1887
	(c) Minority	:	225
	(d) Others	:	392
	(e) Male Population	:	1483
	(f) Female Population	:	1532

Occupational Status

1.	BPL Card Holder	:	202
2.	Antodaya card	:	57
3.	Total number of families with Agricultural occupation	:	406
4.	Landless families	:	10
5.	Old age Pension Holder	:	78
6.	Annapurnna Card Holder	:	13
8.	SHG	:	23

Different Govt. Offices/Institutions

1.	Primary School	:	01
2.	High School	:	01
3.	I.C.D.S.	:	03
4.	Panchayat Office	:	01
5.	Sub-Health centre	:	01
6.	Electric Line	:	5.75 KM
7.	B.L.W. Store	:	01

Source of Irrigation

1.	L.I. Scheme	:	05
2.	High Power L.I.	:	01

Road Communication

1.	Brick Soaling Road	:	3.5 Km
2.	Pucca Road	:	2.5 Km
3.	Katcha Road	:	6 Km

Source of Drinking Water

1.	Tube – Well	:	35
2.	Sanitary – Well	:	09
3.	Mark – 2/3	:	09

Source: Chhataria Gram Panchayat Office.

Table 5.123: Age Group Composition

Age Group	*Percentage of*		
	Vill. – I	*Vill. – II*	*Combined*
15 – 24Yrs	11.11%	12.96%	12.22%
25 – 34 Yrs	25%	27.78%	26.67%

35 – 44 Yrs	38.89%	35.19%	36.67%
45 – 54 Yrs	16.67%	14.81%	15.56%
55 – 64 Yrs	5.55%	5.56%	5.55%
Above – 65 Yrs	2.78%	3.7%	3.33%

Source: Field Survey, 2007.

From the above table and bar diagram can be said that majority respondent was of age group of 35 to 44 years. here were 3.33% respondent who were more than 65 years The percentage of farmers above 65-years is very low which show That the working ability has came down after 65-years.

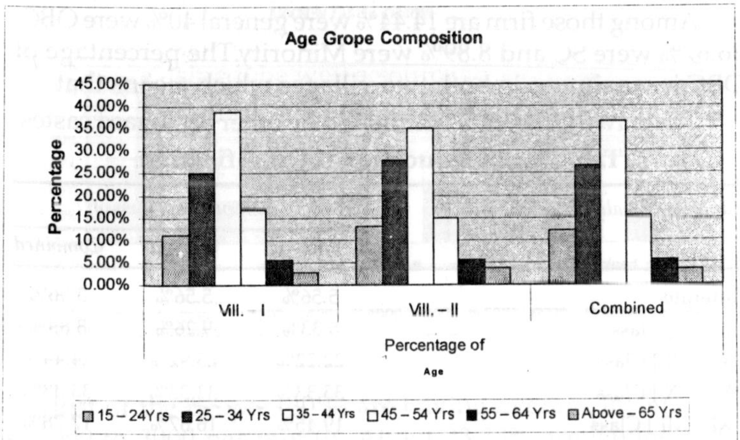

Table 5.123: Caste Status

Caste	*Percentage of*		
	Vill. – I	*Vill. – II*	*Combined*
General	13.89%	14.82%	14.44%
OBC	41.67%	38.89%	40%
SC	36.11%	37.03%	36.67%
Minority	8.33%	9.26%	8.89%

Source: Field Survey.

Table 5.125: Family Belongs to APL/BPL

Family	*Percentage of*		
	Vill. – I	*Vill. – II*	*Combined*
BPL	27.78%	25.92%	26.67%
APL	72.22%	74.08%	73.33%

Source: Field Survey.

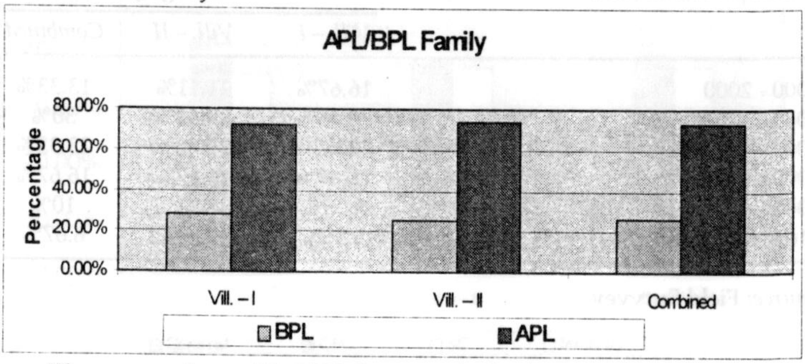

There are about 73.33% farmers belongs to APL and 26.67% farmers belong to BPL that means approximately one fourth of the total farmers of these village are lie below poverty line.

Table 5.126: Land Holding (in Hectares)

Land Holding (in Hectares)	*Percentage of*		
	Vill. – I	*Vill. – II*	*Combined*
Land Less	11.11%	5.56%	7.78%
00 – 0.4	22.22%	12.96%	16.67%
0.4 – 0.8	38.89%	44.44%	42.22%
0.8 – 1.2	19.45%	24.08%	22.22%
Above – 1.2	8.33%	12.96%	11.11%

Source: Field Survey.

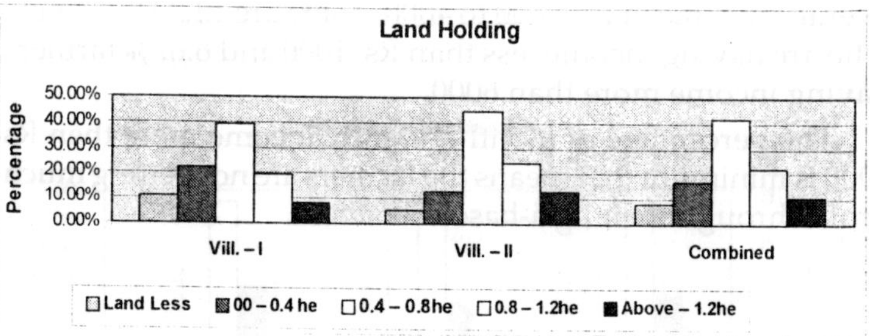

There are about 7.78% land less families, Maximum number of farmers (about 42.22%) are having land about 0.8 to 1.2 (0.4 – 0.8 ha). A very less number about 11.11% are having land on are average of 0.8 to 1.2%.

Although maximum people of these villages are engaged in agriculture but the percentage of land holding above 1.2 hectares is minimum that means the number of large farmer is very low. Marginal and medium farmers are found in the study area.

Table 5.127: Type of Cultivation Land Holding

TYPE	*Percentage of*		
	Vill. – I	*Vill. – II*	*Combined*
Only own	66.67%	66.67%	66.67%
Only Leased	11.11%	9.26%	10%
Own and Leased both	22.22%	24.07%	23.33%

Source: Field Survey.

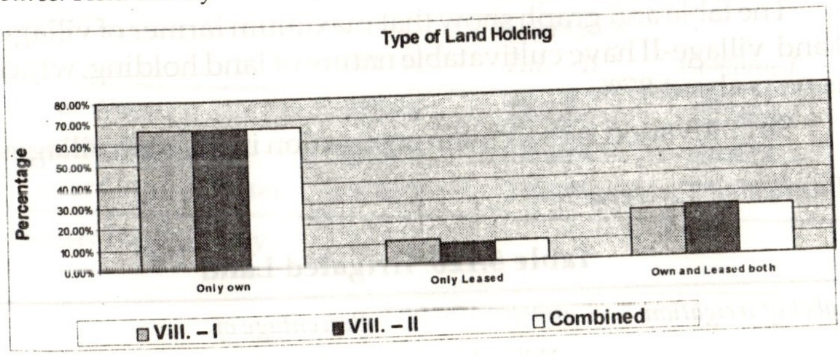

Majority of farmers are cultivating on this own land about 66.67%. A very less percentage that is about 10% is used to cultivate on leased land.

The cultivators in the both villages hold own land, few of them have taken lease land for extending their economic activity related to agriculture.

Table 5.133: Seeds used for Cultivation

Govt. of Dept.	*Percentage of*		
	Vill. – I	*Vill. – II*	*Combined*
Local	11.11%	7.41%	8.89%
HYV	63.89%	72.22%	68.89%
Local and HYV both	25%	20.37%	22.22%

Source: Field Survey.

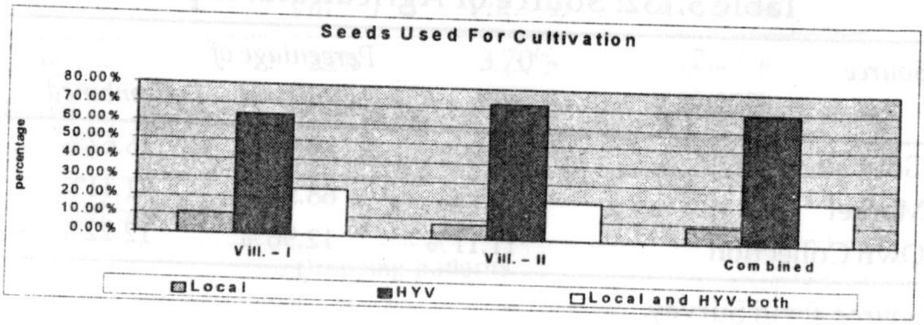

It was found that about 68.89% farmer uses HYV seed and only 8.89% uses local varieties about 22.22% uses both local and HYV seeds. It means that farmers are like to grow mainly HYV.

Table 5.134: Fertilizer Used

Fertilizer	*Percentage of*		
	Vill. – I	*Vill. – II*	*Combined*
Only organic	11.11%	5.56%	7.78%
Chemical and Organic both	88.89%	94.44%	92.22%

Source: Field Survey.

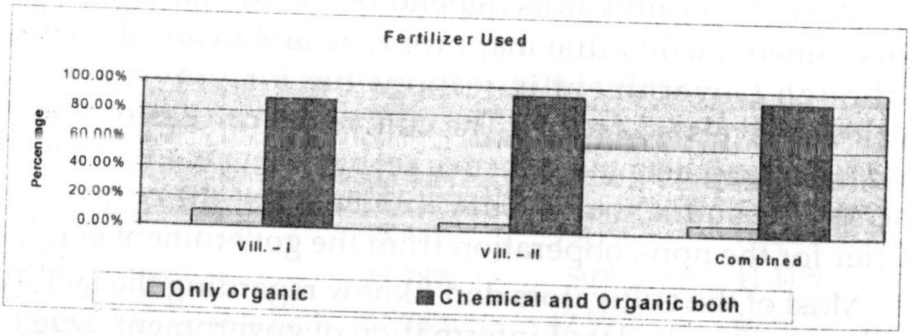

Graphical Presentation of Fertilizer Used

From the above table we say that most of the farmer (92.22%)

Results

use both chemical and organic fertilizer. The percentage of farmer (7.78%) is very low who use only organic fertilizer

There is a good trend for using the organic fertilizer in the study area. It is the good symptom to the Indian agriculture that the cultivators are being habituated with the organic farming.

Table 5.135: Other farming practice by the farmers (in Vill – I and Vill – I in Combined)

Farming	*Percentage*
Dairy	11.11%
Poultry	7.78%
Fishery	4.44%
Dairy and Poultry both	20%
Dairy and Fishery both	7.78%
Poultry and Fishery	6.67%
Dairy, Poultry and Fishery all	42.22%

Source: Field Survey.

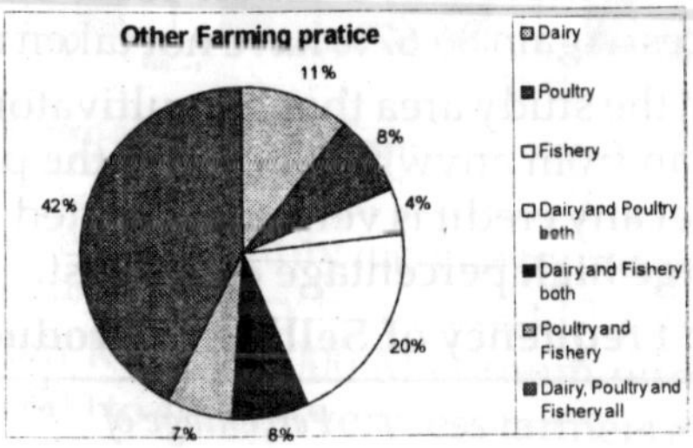

Dairy is a most common enterprise among all the enterprises which is 42.22% including dairy, poultry and fish farm, where as 11.11% farmer practice only dairy farm.

So it can be said that dairy is the second alternative choice to the cultivators followed by agriculture.

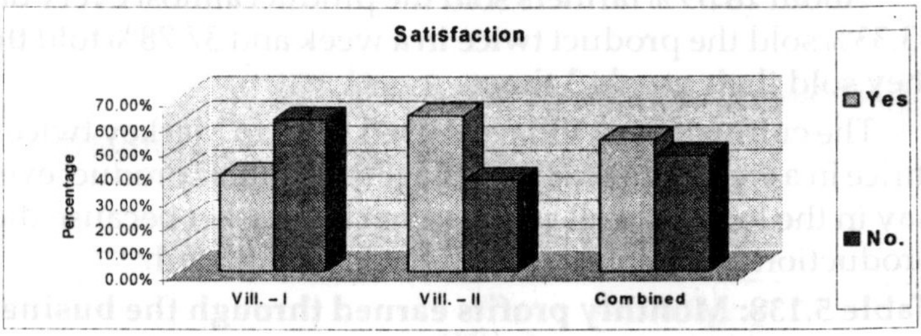

About 53.33% farmers are satisfied with the profit which they earn. About 46.67% are not satisfied it may be due to les profit.

The study shows that most of the cultivators of V-II are satisfied with their agri-business but the least percentage of people is satisfied with their agricultural activity.

Cropping Pattern

Almost all farmers are practicing mixed cropping when they cultivate vegetables simultaneously they cultivate a number of vegetables in the same field like cucumber, cauliflower and tomato are cultivated in a same field. But in case of rice only mono cropping is followed.

Organic Fertilizer Organic Consumption

Almost all farmers' uses cow dung as organic fertilizer. Some other commonly used organic fertilizers are oilcakes, bio fertilizer, FYM etc.

Organic Pesticide Consumption

No farmer is using organic pesticide due to lack of proper information and awareness.

Availability of Market

Most of the farmers depend on more than one market for selling of goods. When they are producing the goods in small amount they depend on local market when it is sold in large amount, the products are sold in Urban market like Agatrala or Udaipur.

The buyer of the vegetables is either local people or whole seller where as incase of rice whole sellers are the buyer. Some middlemen are found in the study area, and they are concentrated in V-I due to their low income

Distance

The nearest market from the study area is between 1-2 Kms and it is 3-7 kms for urban market (Udaipur) and if they want to sell their product at city market (Agartala), they have to cover 46-50 kms. They carry out their products either by bicycle, auto or zeep. The condition of road is also not so bad.

Support for Marketing

No support has been provided by government for better marketing of goods. For this reason they are exploited by the middlemen and deprived from the reasonable price of their goods.

Training

Through some of the farmers receive various types of training but they never received their how to get more profit through marketing of agricultural goods.

Utilization of Profit

The profit earned through this business is utilized in many ways these are:–

(*a*) daily consumption of goods in terms of other food materials cereals, oil spices etc.

(*b*) Education for their children.

(*c*) Health expenditure.

(*d*) There is also an intensity of savings in the bank.

Major Findings

1. Most of the farmers are small scale farmers. Almost all of them are selling their surplus goods in the market.

ownership of the programme. States have been requested to launch a concerted campaign of mass mobilization of mothers.

Under the above mentioned circumstances some suggestion can be put forward for the overall development of the school and on analyzing the above factors it is recommended that,

1. In Adwaita Malla Barman J.B. School under Melaghar R.D. Block, it has been seen that there is a common class room of all students belonging to class-I to Class-V and there is no separate room for teacher. Under the above situation it is recommended that separate class room should be made for the students belonging to separate classes and there should be one staff room for teachers.
2. Ongoing through the above school it has been found that in every school Kitchen room is closely attached with the class room which is hampering the studies of children who are reading in the said school. Under the circumstance it is recommended that Kitchen room should be made far away from class room.
3. It has been seen that Government has provide LPG facility for cooking for every school but it has recommended only Rs. 0.05 for egg and vegetable and Rs. 0.10 for Khichuri, Rice and Vegetable, the amount has been found very short for running LPG cylinder. As a result to meet the expenses, food are seem to be cooked through which is not only healthy but also environment friendly? Under the above circumstances it is recommended that the allocation fund for each child should be increased so as to meet the cost of LPG.
4. The rate of allocation under the above schemes is found to be short in compare to the market rate. So the market service community should be formed and it is assumed that the correct rate of commodities will be allocated.
5. More number of worker or helper should be appointed, as it is not possible for a person to serve

at least 100 numbers of children on an average.

6. It has been seen that every student is not getting utensils as said according to the schemes, so a monitoring cell may be created.
7. The quality of food supply should be according to the increasing age as well as of classes.

The present condition of farmers is not good due to the less profit earned through the agro-based business which covers the significant part of their regular life. If the marketing facilities are improved and problems in market are solved then the farmer will get more benefit and can be able to improve their socio-economic condition. For this purpose a systematic strategy should be prepared.

They need proper knowledge, information, agricultural equipment, training for batter marketing facilities etc. For this Government should come forward to help them.

Lastly – "without food no one can live and without farmer no food material with produce".

21.Dantwala, M.L., (1978), 'Future of Institutional Reform and Technological Change and in Indiaa Agrucultural Development', Economic and Political Weekly, Vol-12.

Dantwala, M.L., Sethi, Harsh and Visaria, Parveen (1998), *Social Change through Voluntary Action*, Sage Publication, New Delhi.

Das D.K. (ed.) (1999), *Social Sector and Development Experiences and Challenges*, New Delhi: Deep and Deep Publications.

24.Das Gupta, Partha. An Inquiry into well being and Destitution; Oxford University Press, New Delhi, 1993.

Das, B.N. and Sarkar, A.K., "Rural Area Development: Karnal Area: A Case Study", *Indian Journal of Regional Science*, Vol. IV. No.2, 1972.

Datta, Anindita and Sinha, Sachidanand (1997), Gender disparities in social well beings: An overview, *Indian Journal of Gender Studies*, Vol. 4, No. 1.

Datt, Ruddar, Sundharam, K.P.M. (2000), "Indian Economy", S.Chand & Co. Ltd., New Delhi-110055.

Devadas, R. P. (1999). *Women and Development. Centre for Women's Studies*, Avinashilingam Deemed University.

Dhar, Aarti, Roll out better life for women: study (the bidi workers have no access to schemes), *The Hindu*, May 2,2005, Hyderabad.

Dodkey, M.P. (1999). SHGs and micro credit sustaining rural women, *Social Welfare*, Vol. 45, No.12.

East India Human Development Report; National Council of Applied Economic Research; Oxford University Press, New Delhi, 2004, pp. 255-335.

Economic and Political Weekly Research Foundation (1994), Social indicators for development for India: Inter state disparities, *Economic and Political Weekly*, Vol. XXIX, No. 21.

Economic Survey (2004-05) (http://indiabudget.nic.in)

EFA 2000 Assessment: India Country Report (MHRD & NIEPA, New Delhi).

Esman, Milton and Uphoff, N. *Local Organisations for Rural Development: Analysis of Asian Experience*. Springfield: NTIS, 1974.

Festinger L. and Katz D. (eds.) 1953. *Research Methods in Behavioural Sciences*. Holt, Rinehart and Winston Inc., New York.

Fisher, C.S. (1982), *To dwell among Friends: Personal Networks in Towns and City*, University of Chicago Press, Chicago.

Fisher, T. and Sriram, M.S. (2002) *Beyond Micro-Credit: Putting Development Back into Micro-Finance*, New Delhi: Vistaar Publications.

Franda, Marcus (1979): *Small is politics: Organisational Alternatives in India's Rural Development*, Wiley Eastern Limited, New Delhi.

Friedmann. J.R. and Weaver. C. (1979) *Territory and Function: The Evolution of Regional Planning*, London.

Friedmann, J.R. (1972) 'A general theory of polarized development', in Hansen (Ed), *Growth Centres in Regional Economic Development*, New York.

Gaikwad, V.R. (1969): *Panchayati Raj and Bureaucracy in Community Development*, National Institute of Rural Development, , Hyderabad.

Gangrade, K.D. (1985) *Social networks and Social Work: Crisis management in Indian Families*, Northern Book Centre, New Delhi.

Gangulee, N.N. (1984): *Problems of Rural India*, Mittal Publications, Delhi.

Gehlawat, J.K. and Kant (1988): *Strategies for Rural Development*, Arnold Publishers India, New Delhi.

Ghate, Prabhu (1984): *Direct Attacks on Rural Poverty*, Concept Publishing Company, New Delhi.

Ghosh, Jayati, Gender – a left priority, 2004, http://www.indiatogether.org

Goode W. J. and Hatt P. H. 1981. *Methods in Social Research*, McGraw Hill Book Company, Singapore.

Government of West Bengal, Planning and Development Department: Economic Review of different years.

Govinda, R. *India Education Report: A Profile of Basic Education*, National Institute of Educational Planning and Administration (2002), Oxford University Press, New Delhi.

Guha, R., (1994), *Social Ecology*, Oxford University Press, New Delhi.

Guhan, S. (1995), Social expenditure in the union budget: 1991-96, *Economic and Political Weekly*, Vol. 30, No. 18, and 19.

Gurumoorthy,T.R. (2000). Self Help Groups empower rural women, *Kurukshetra*, Vol. 48, No. 5.

Hassard, J., (1993), *Sociology and Organization Theory*, Cambridge University Press.

Head, W.A. (1979) "Community Development in Post-Industrial Society: Myth and Reality," in D.A. Chekki, (ed.), (1979), *Community Development: Theory and Method of Planned Change*, Vikas Publishing House, New Delhi.

Hermansen, T. (1972) 'Development poles and related theories' in Hansen (Ed.) *Growth Centres in Regional Economic Development*, Now York.

National Common Minimum Programme of the Government of India, May 2004 (http://pmindia.nic.in/cmp.htm)

National Council of Educational Research and Training (1998). Sixth All India Educational Survey, Volume 1-Educational Facilities in Rural and Urban Areas. New Delhi.

National Human Development Report, 2001 (http://planningcommission.nic.in/reports).

National Institute of Rural Development, 1999, India Rural Development Report; (Ed.) R.C. Choudhury and S.Rajakutty.

National Institute of Rural Development, Hyderabad (1979): *Rural Development in India: Some Facets.*

Paulchaudhury, D., *Women Welfare & Development*, Inter-India Publications.

Pradhan, Basanta K., Roy, P.K.; Saluja, M.R. and Venkatraman, Shanta (2000), Rural-Urban disparities, income distribution, expenditure pattern and social sector, *Economic and Political Weekly*, Vol. XXXV, No. 28 and 29.

Prasad, R.R. (2001), Social Development: Meaning, Concept and Strategies, in Social Development in Rural Areas: Strategies and Development, a Reading Material from Centre for Social Development, NIRD, Hyderabad (Mimeograph).

PROBE (1999). Public Report On Basic Education in India. The PROBE team in Association with Centre for Development Economics. Oxford University Press, New Delhi.

Public Infromation-2006.

Ray, Singh D.K., (ed.), (2001), *Social Development and Empowerment of Marginalised Groups: Perspectives and Strategies*, Sage Publications, New Delhi.

Roberts, K.W.S. 1980 "Price Independent Welfare Prescriptions", *Journal of Public Economics*, 13.

Rothschild, Michael and Joseph E. Stiglitz, 1970 "Increasing Risk: 1. A Definition", *Journal of Economic Theory* 2(3) September.

Rout, H.S. (1998), India's Health Sector: Past and Present., *Vision*, Vol. XVIII, No. 1-2.

Roy, P. and Patil, B.R., *Manual for Block Level Planning*, The MacMillan Company of India, Delhi, 1977.

Rural Development: Sector Policy Paper, Published by the World Bank, 1975.

Samal, B., Institutional Credit flow to West Bengal agriculture: revisited, *Indian Journal of Agricultural Economics*, Vol-57 (3), pp. 546-559, 2002.

Sarma, E. A. S., (2004): 'Is Rural Economy Breaking Down? Farmers' Suicides in Andhra Pradesh', *Economic and Political Weekly,* July 10.

Saxena, N.C. (2000), How Have the Poor Done? Mid Term Review of Ninth Plan: Commentary, *Economic and Political Weekly,* Vol. XXXV, No. 41.

Selected Educational Statistics (1998). Ministry of Human Resource Development, Government of India, New Delhi.

Sen, L.K. and others, (1975), Growth Centres in Raichur: An Integrated Area Development Plan for a District in Karnataka. NICD, Hyderabad.

Sengupta, Jayshree, The Disappearing crafts, http: // www.observerindia.com

Sengupta, Keya (1999), Trends in educational expenditure and its impact on Indian economy, in D.K. Das (ed.), *Social Sector and Development,* Deep and Deep Publications, New Delhi.

Shah, Anil C. and Sudarsahn, Iyengar (1998), The Contribution of NGO's to development: Some issues and a case study, in a book on *Social Change through Voluntary Action,* Dantwala, M.L. Harsh Sethi and Parvin Vasaria (Ed.), Sage Publications, New Delhi.

Shrimal, Mohan Lal (1985): *Land Reforms: Promise and Performances,* Metropolitan Book Co. Pvt. New Delhi.

Singh, Katar (1999) "Rural Development"- Principles, Polices and Mangement", Sage Publication India Pvt Ltd.

Singh, Jashar (1974): *The Green Revolution in India: How Green it is,* Vishal Publications, Kurukshetra.

Singh, Katar (2001): *Rural Development: Principles, Policies and Management,* Sage Publications, New Delhi.

Singh, Bhupinder and Neeti Mahanti (Ed.) (1997): *Tribal Policy in India,* Inter-India Publications, New Delhi.

Sonamura. I.S Office.

Swami H.R., Gupta, B.P. (2005-5006), *Rural Development and Co-operation in India,* Indus Valley Publications, Jaipur-New Delhi

Tandon, Dr. Rajesh (1995), " STATE PANCHYAT ACTS, A Critical Review", VANI-Voluntary Action Network India, H-17/1, Malviya Nagar, New Delhi 110017.

Taylor, Carl C. et. al. (1967): India's Roots of Democracy: A Sociological Analysis of Rural India's Experiences in Planned Development since independence. Orient Longman, New Delhi.

Thakur, Shrinivas Y. (1985): *Rural Industrialisation in India,* Sterling Publishers, New Delhi.

Thakur, Devendra (1986): *Rurai Development and Planning in India*, Deep & Deep Publications, New Delhi.

W.K.D. Davies: "The Ranking of service Centres: A Critical Review," *Transactions and Papers Institute of British Geographers*, No. 18-19, 1952.

Wanmali, Sudhir (1976) 'Regional Development, regional planning and the hierarchy of towns', *Bombay Geographical Magazine*, Vol. 15.

Wanmali, Sudhir and Ghosh, A. (1975) 'Pattern of distribution of consumer goods in rural India', *Management and Labour Studies*, Vol. 1.

Wanmali, Sudhir and Khan, Waheeduddin (1970) 'Role of location in regional planning with particular reference to the provision of social facilities, *Behavioural Sciences and Community Development*, Vol. 4.

Wanmali, Sudhir: *Service Centres in Rural India*, 1983; B. R. Publishing Corporation; Delhi.

Websites:

Williamson. J.G., "Regional Inequality and Process of National Development", *Economic Development and Cultural Change*, 13, No. 4. Pt, 2. 1965.

Wolf, Jr. Charles., (1955), 'Institutions and Economic Development', *American Economic Review.*

www.google.com

www.india.org

www.rural.nic.in

www.ruraltripura.nic.in

www.tripura.nic.in

www.yahoo.com

Yojna, a journal on Rural Development, {all edition of 2006}.